D0186859

Opening Dialogue: Understanding the
Dynamics of Language and Learning in
the English Classroom
MARTIN NYSTRAND with ADAM
GAMORAN, ROBERT KACHUR, and
CATHERINE PRENDERGAST

Reading Across Cultures: Teaching
Literature in a Diverse Society
THERESA ROGERS and
ANNA O. SOTER, Editors

"You Gotta Be the Book": Teaching
Engaged and Reflective Reading
with Adolescents
JEFFREY D. WILHELM

Just Girls: Hidden Literacies and
Life in Junior High
MARGARET J. FINDERS

The First R: Every Child's Right to Read
MICHAEL F. GRAVES, PAUL VAN DEN
BROEK, and BARBARA M. TAYLOR, Editors

Exploring Blue Highways:
Literacy Reform, School Change, and
the Creation of Learning Communities
JOBETH ALLEN, MARILYNN CARY, and
LISA DELGADO, Coordinators

Envisioning Literature:
Literary Understanding
and Literature Instruction
JUDITH A. LANGER

Teaching Writing as Reflective Practice
GEORGE HILLOCKS, JR.

Talking Their Way into Science:
Hearing Children's Questions and
Theories, Responding with Curricula
KAREN GALLAS

Whole Language Across the
Curriculum: Grades 1, 2, 3
SHIRLEY C. RAINES, Editor

The Administration and Supervision of
Reading Programs, SECOND EDITION
SHELLEY B. WEPNER, JOAN T. FEELEY,
and DOROTHY S. STRICKLAND, Editors

No Quick Fix: Rethinking
Literacy Programs in America's
Elementary Schools
RICHARD L. ALLINGTON and
SEAN A. WALMSLEY, Editors

Unequal Opportunity:
Learning to Read in the U.S.A.
JILL SUNDAY BARTOLI

Nonfiction for the Classroom:
Milton Meltzer on Writing, History,
and Social Responsibility
Edited and with an Introduction by
E. WENDY SAUL

When Children Write: Critical
Re-Visions of the Writing Workshop
TIMOTHY LENSMIRE

Dramatizing Literature in Whole
Language Classrooms, SECOND EDITION
JOHN WARREN STEWIG and
CAROL BUEGE

The Languages of Learning:
How Children Talk, Write,
Dance, Draw, and Sing Their
Understanding of the World
KAREN GALLAS

Partners in Learning: Teachers and
Children in Reading Recovery
CAROL A. LYONS, GAY SU PINNELL,
and DIANE E. DEFORD

Social Worlds of Children
Learning to Write in an
Urban Primary School
ANNE HAAS DYSON

(Continued)

LANGUAGE AND LITERACY SERIES (*continued*)

The Politics of Workplace Literacy:
A Case Study
   SHERYL GREENWOOD GOWEN

Inside/Outside:
Teacher Research and Knowledge
   MARILYN COCHRAN-SMITH
   and SUSAN L. LYTLE

Literacy Events in a
Community of Young Writers
   YETTA M. GOODMAN
   and SANDRA WILDE, Editors

Whole Language Plus:
Essays on Literacy in the
United States and New Zealand
   COURTNEY B. CAZDEN

Process Reading and Writing:
A Literature-Based Approach
   JOAN T. FEELEY,
   DOROTHY S. STRICKLAND,
   and SHELLEY B. WEPNER, Editors

The Child as Critic:
Teaching Literature in Elementary
and Middle Schools, THIRD EDITION
   GLENNA DAVIS SLOAN

The Triumph of Literature/
The Fate of Literacy: English in the
Secondary School Curriculum
   JOHN WILLINSKY

The Child's Developing Sense of Theme:
Responses to Literature
   SUSAN S. LEHR

Literacy for a Diverse Society:
Perspectives, Practices, and Policies
   ELFRIEDA H. HIEBERT, Editor

The Complete Theory-to-Practice
Handbook of Adult Literacy:
Curriculum Design and
Teaching Approaches
   RENA SOIFER, MARTHA IRWIN,
   BARBARA CRUMRINE, EMO HONZAKI,
   BLAIR SIMMONS, and DEBORAH YOUNG

just girls

hidden literacies and life in junior high

margaret j. finders

NCTE

National Council of Teachers of English   Urbana, Illinois

Teachers College   Columbia University   New York and London

Published by Teachers College Press, 1234 Amsterdam Avenue, New York, NY 10027

Portions of this book appeared in *Written Communication*, volume 13, number 1. Copyright Sage Publications (1996). Reprinted with permission from *Written Communication*.

Portions of Chapter 3 appeared in *Anthropology and Education Quarterly*, volume 27, number 1. Copyright American Anthropological Association (1996). Reprinted with permission from *Anthropology & Education Quarterly*.

Library of Congress Cataloging-in-Publication Data

Finders, Margaret.
   Just girls : hidden literacies and life in junior high / Margaret Finders.
        p.   cm. — (Language and literacy series)
     Includes bibliographical references and index.
      ISBN 0-8077-3560-4 (pbk.). — ISBN 0-8077-3561-2 (cloth)
      1. Adolescence.   2. Literacy—Social aspects.   3. Girls—Social networks.   4. Junior high school students—Attitudes.
     5. Educational sociology.   I. Title.   II. Series: Language and literacy series (New York, N.Y.)
     LB1135.F496   1996
     305.2'35'08352—dc20   96-2930

ISBN 0-8077-3560-4 (paper)
ISBN 0-8077-3561-2 (cloth)
NCTE stock number 25387

Printed on acid-free paper
Manufactured in the United States of America

03   8 7 6 5

Contents

Foreword by Linda Christian-Smith   vii
Acknowledgments   xi

INTRODUCTION   1

CHAPTER 1 *"When You're in Junior High, Everything's Different"*   6
Northern Hills Community School District   6
Sociocultural Perspectives on Literacy   8
Adolescent Girls: Shifting Conceptions   11
"Just Regular Girls": Presenting Social Roles   14
Official Expectations and Literate Underlife   24
Language Arts at Northern Hills Junior High School   26
"What Junior High Is All About": Social Roles and
    the Discourse of Adolescence   28

CHAPTER 2 *Entering Adolescence: Literacy
and Allegiance in Junior High*   31
"A Sense of Belonging": Social Roles and
    the Yearbook "Event"   31
Social Boundaries: The Queens and the Cookies   33
"Sign Mine": Constructing Identity and
    Claiming Allegiance   40
Patrolling the Borders: Literacy as Ritual of Exclusion   43
Embracing Adolescence: The Yearbook as Process
    and Object   45

CHAPTER 3 *Literacy and the Social Queens*   48
The Lifeworld of the Social Queens   48
Literate Practices   54
Literate Underlife   55
School-Sanctioned Literacies   71
Summary and Conclusion   79

CHAPTER 4 *Literacy and the Tough Cookies*   83
The Lifeworld of the Tough Cookies   83

Literate Practices   90
Literacies Beyond the Sanctions   91
School-Sanctioned Literacies   104
Summary and Conclusions   114

CHAPTER 5   *Viewing and Reviewing Classroom Roles*   *116*
Rendering Visible "Terministic Screens"   117
Myths of Student-Centered Pedagogy   118
Myths of Adolescence   121
"They're All Good Girls": Viewing Classroom Roles   123
Implications for Pedagogy: Revising Our Roles   125
Implications for Further Research   128
Just Girls   130

References   133
Index   139
About the Author   145

Foreword

There has been a steadily increasing body of research about girls, their subcultures and literacies since Angela McRobbie's landmark studies appeared in 1978. McRobbie's study (1978b) of white working-class teenage girls at a Birmingham, England youth club identified a "culture of femininity" composed of close friends and organized around domestic duties, consumption of goods and services, personal life, and romance. Many of these girls received their information about being feminine from the popular British teen magazine *Jackie*, which McRobbie (1978a) also analyzed as to the ways femininities are shaped through text and images. This interest in how popular texts constitute and reconstitute the social identities of young women readers at school and home continues to be explored in my own work (1990, 1993, in review), as well as that of Pam Gilbert and Sandra Taylor (1991), Meredith Cherland (1994), and now in Margaret Finders' *Just Girls*.

In *Just Girls*, the focus is the role of literacy in the social development of Tiffany, Angie, Lauren, Dottie, and Cleo, academically successful 12 and 13 year-old girls of middle- and working-class and Euro-American background residing in the rural Midwest. Finders construes literacy more widely than in previous research. Signing year books, writing notes and bathroom graffiti, reading "teen zines," (magazines) and doing homework together are literacy events just as important as reading novels and short stories and writing in classroom response journals. For Finders, girls' literate competence is constituted in the interstices between the latter "official" classroom literacy activities, the peer group, and what Finders terms girls' "literate underlife" of contesting official expectations. Finders also suggests that literacy is more than a set of private practices and that more than literate competence is developed with the flip of a page or stroke of a pen. Literacy is eminently a social event that constructs social identities, positions girls within their peer groups, and demarcates social boundaries between adults and children and school social groups. *Just Girls* further demonstrates Baker and Luke's (1991) contention that literacy is a significant form of cultural capital that constructs and regulates subcultural and class identity and power.

Finders provides a highly nuanced portrait of the world of the "social queens"—Tiffany, Angie, and Lauren—and the "tough cookies"—Dottie and Cleo—and their families during seventh grade at Northern Hills Junior High School. For the middle-class queens, this is a time when socializing is very important and the friendship group rules. Another picture emerges from the working-class cookies; for them, it is a time of peer group marginalization and retreating into oneself. Literacy is central to all of this, in the formation of the social selves described in *Just Girls*. It is well-documented that many women's sense of self is organized around relationships (e.g., Belenky, Clinchy, Goldberger, & Tarule, 1986; Gilligan, Lyons, & Hanmer, 1990). *Just Girls* breaks new ground by indicating how self and relationships are constituted and reconstituted through friendship, family, school networks, and the role of literacy. Student's experiences are further analyzed in relation to larger patterns of culture and power. Yet to regard self and female early adolescence in a unified way is a mistake. By entering the world of the queens and the cookies, Finders demonstrates that young women's selves are diverse and that experiental background diversifies beyond race, class, and gender.

Many readers may find themselves in the universe of the queens and cookies. Although I did not live in a trailer court like Cleo and Dottie, my background resembles theirs. During junior high school, I was caught between the differing cultures and demands of school and my working-class family. While family income made possible the move into the middle class, I did not possess the cultural capital of a Tiffany or Lauren, so I remained between two worlds. Other similarities between myself and the cookies emerged in our shared beliefs about schooling and literacy at that time: "Kissing up" to teachers for easy grades is fraudulent, sharing ideas is cheating, meaningless and boring assignments still have to be done, school is for academics—and success there was the ticket to economic security and power. Like Dottie, I regarded literacy as a solitary practice and endowed texts with great authority. I was also like Cleo with my interest in women's issues and my attitude toward books as showing me the world beyond home and family. Rather than peers, our families were our support networks, especially mothers and other female relatives.

Many readers may also have encountered social queens like Tiffany, Lauren, and Angie who are so tied to their friendship groups that they seem to function as a single entity. *Just Girls* suggests that literacy is the tie that binds them together. The queens wrote notes to friends and yearbook messages to hold their friendship group together—and to exclude others such as the cookies and adults. Literacy was also used for entertainment and an antidote to boredom in school. For the queens and cookies, literacy constructs particular forms of self. Whereas the cookies presented studious and self-sufficient selves, the queens projected public images of niceness and helpfulness but expressed resistance to school in their notes critiquing classroom literacy practices. Although capable, the queens did only enough work to get by and were nonchalant about academics. Instead, the queens focused their efforts on the teen zines *Sassy* and *YM*, which provided information on their main concerns: how to look, act and be a popular girl.

Just Girls goes a long way to seriously question many of the beliefs about young adolescents and current student-centered and literacy education practices in middle-level schools aimed at developing comfort zones and belonginess through cooperative learning, writing response groups, and expanded free choices for students. Adolescence emerges here as socially situated rather than biological; students stage behaviors to meet assumptions about adolescence. In *Just Girls*, participation in response and cooperative learning groups is influenced by the codes of the two friendship groups, which may define this as social time or as such an invasion of privacy that students are further silenced. The cookies and the queens demonstrate that personal responses and choices are not really free, but are constrained by the power structures of classrooms, peer groups, and families, as well as larger socioeconomic and political factors. Finders further suggests that "a pedagogy built on comfort, built on students' experiences, will, of course, continue to privilege those who feel most at home in the classroom"—usually students from Euro-American and middle-class backgrounds. Throughout *Just Girls*, students' allegiances to peers interfere with high levels of intellectual engagement.

Just Girls graphically documents for middle level and literacy educators the consequences of reducing teachers' goals to making students comfortable instead of intellectually challenging them; of nurturing connectedness to peers rather than to adults; and of privileging niceness and cooperation over other characteristics that young adolescent girls possess. Adolescence is a crucial time for young women, when families and schools should aim at transforming them from "just girls" to extraordinary young women.

—*Linda Christian-Smith*

REFERENCES

Baker, C. D., & Luke, A. (1991). *Toward a critical sociology of reading pedagogy.* Amsterdam: John Benjamins.

Belenky, M. F., Clinchy, B. M., Goldberger, N. R., & Tarule, J. (1986). *Women's ways of knowing: The development of self, voice and mind.* New York: Basic Books.

Cherland, M. (1994). *Private practices: Girls reading fiction and constructing identity.* London: Taylor and Francis.

Christian-Smith, L. K. (1990). *Becoming a woman through romance.* New York: Routledge.

Christian-Smith, L. K. (1993). *Texts of desire: Essays on fiction, femininity and schooling.* London: The Falmer Press.

Christian-Smith, L. K. (in review). More than crime on her mind: Nancy Drew as woman hero. In D. Jones & T. Watkins (Eds.), *The heroic figure in children's popular culture.* Hamden, CT: Garland Press.

Gilbert, P., & Taylor, S. (1991). *Fashioning the feminine: Girls, popular culture and schooling.* Sydney: Allen & Unwin.

Gilligan, C., Lyons, N., & Hanmer, T. J. (1990). *Making connections: The relational worlds of adolescent girls at Emma Willard School.* Cambridge, MA: Harvard University Press.

McRobbie, A. (1978a). *Jackie: An ideology of adolescent femininity.* Stencilled Occasional Paper. Birmingham, UK: The Centre for Contemporary Cultural Studies.

McRobbie, A. (1978b). Working class girls and the culture of femininity. In Women's Studies Group (Eds.), *Women take issue* (pp. 97–108). London: Hutchinson.

Acknowledgments

I owe a debt of gratitude to The University of Iowa for providing a rich opportunity to learn from some of the finest scholars in literacy education. I am deeply appreciative of Carolyn Colvin, Anne DiPardo, Jim Marshall, Bonnie Sunstein, and Mary Trachsel whose insightful reflections offered guidance from initial conception to completion of this project. I wish to thank Julie Cheville and Cynthia Lewis who offered generous support and critical response. Their probing questions made this work stronger. Thank you also to Jim Davis, Walter Cannon, Kerry Evans, Frank Hubbard and the many Iowa Writing Project participants who provided intellectual stimulation throughout my teaching and who continue to offer collegial support.

Of course, without the participants—the cookies and the queens, their parents, and their teachers—this work would not be possible. I appreciate their willingness to share a bit of their lives with me.

Finally, thank you to my daughters Anna and Sally, who teetered on the edge of adolescence, and to Jim Finders—each offered support, direction, and opportunities for reflection and escape throughout this project.

Introduction

After spending 13 years at the front of a language arts classroom, I decided to move to the back where it seemed to me some very interesting literacy work was going on: a note secretly passed, a magazine carefully concealed between the pages of a science workbook. Around the fringes of my seventh-grade classroom, I had glimpses into a literate culture that was not part of any official curriculum. Everhart (1983) begins his book by asking, "What are the early adolescent years (12 to 15) about?" After spending 13 years teaching 13-year-olds, I still had more questions than answers.

I wanted to better understand the rules and rituals that accompany entry into adolescence. I wanted to explore the secretive literate practices that lurked about my classroom. I knew I had to take on a role far removed from that of a teacher in order to tap into what I later came to refer to as "literate underlife," those practices designed to contest official expectations. To more fully understand the perspective of the early adolescent female, I undertook a year-long ethnographic study at one midwestern junior high school from 1992 to 1993. I selected a school district I knew and whose teachers and pedagogy I valued highly. It was my goal as a researcher to enter a school site where the pedagogy was sound, where students actively engaged in reading and writing workshops, and, perhaps most importantly, where students were the center of the curriculum.

I, like Lensmire (1994), thought I would have a different story to tell. I, too, thought it would be "this gratifying story of workshop life" (p. 1). I thought that by selecting as a research site a language arts program where reading and writing were abundant and central, I would write of community and collaboration and inclusion. Yet, after a year of research, I am now less sure of the pedagogy that previously I had embraced so completely.

I met Angie, Tiffany, Lauren, Cleo, and Dottie in May of their sixth-grade year.[1] Their teacher introduced me simply as someone who was interested in learning about their reading and writing. As an interested onlooker in the classroom, I wanted students to view me as different

1

from other adults who held authority in the school. I carefully monitored my interactions with teachers and administrators in school encounters and avoided any situation in which my role might be read as tutor or teacher. I deliberately dressed to distinguish myself from school personnel, most often wearing jeans, a T-shirt, and tennis shoes.

At recess, while students were busy at play, friendship circles became visible. It was easy to pick out the group leaders, Tiffany and Cleo. Since research on adolescence suggests that peer-group relations become more influential as they are distanced from adult supervision (Brooks-Gunn & Reiter, 1990; Brown, 1990; Feldman & Elliott, 1990), I selected Tiffany and her best friends, Angie and Lauren; and Cleo and her best friend Dottie as focal students. I promised the girls confidentiality, and their developing relationships with me soon brought status among their peers and privileged mobility in the school structure: "Oh, she's writing a book about us." Focal students were granted permission to leave study halls to tape interviews with me. During study time in language arts classes, the girls often led me to a library study room to talk privately. Lunch time promised an opportunity to talk in the public presence of their larger circle of friends, both boys and girls.

I accompanied Cleo, Dottie, Angie, Tiffany, and Lauren in their transition from a self-contained sixth-grade classroom into a traditional junior high setting. Over the course of that year, these early adolescents allowed me the opportunity to learn from them, to learn again what it is like to be caught between childhood and adulthood. Their eagerness to share their views, reveal their struggles, and open up their homes to me made this study possible. I think it is fair to say that they are by far my most influential teachers.

The focal students as group members saw their group as distinct from other groups, and each privately expressed a dislike for the other group. This, of course, complicated my movement between groups. At first I tried to avoid being seen by one group in the presence of another, but because of the structure of the school building and the schedule of the school day that was not possible. I was forced to admit openly my interests in each group. I withheld information from focal students who asked about the other group's interests and activities, explaining only that I wanted to learn what being a teenager today was like for each group. While each group explained that I was wasting my time on the other group, they accepted my movement between groups. Aware of my interest in another group, focal students on numerous occasions stated that I needed to listen carefully to them because, as they said, "We do it right. They don't know. We're right." Obviously, from their perspective, they did have it right. Taking on roles as teachers, focal students attempted to teach me how to get along in the adolescent world, and how to do it "right" according to their perspective of what "doing it right" meant.

I spent one year documenting the girls' literate practices both in and out of school. The goal of this project was to document how each event was framed from their point of view. By documenting who was present and where, when, and for whom such events occurred, I attempted to make visible the tacit rules and demands that shape such events and ultimately shape available social roles within particular social circles.

An examination of a group's literacy events led to a richer understanding of the dynamics of social networks. Such a focus demanded an ethnographic approach (Erickson, 1986; Spradley, 1980). Data were obtained by participant observation (Spradley, 1979, 1980) as well as by interviewing and collecting written artifacts of participants. Emphasis was placed on documenting naturally occurring key incidents, specifically literacy events (Heath, 1982). Tagging along with focal students to athletic events and the mall, listening in on their phone conversations, hanging out at slumber parties, and observing them in the cafeteria and hallways as well as during language arts classes, I began to explore what the early adolescent years (12 to 15) are about from the perspective of the early adolescent female.

The sociolinguist James Gee (1990) calls a discourse community an "identity kit" that comes already equipped with ways of seeing, acting, thinking, and talking in the world; yet such a "kit" for the early adolescent is in flux. Secondary school often seems to serve as a marker of entry into adolescence. Thus by virtue of enrollment, seventh graders are at the threshold of adolescence, at a critical juncture in their academic and social development. In September, they face an unfamiliar cultural scene: the junior high school. They are just beginning to negotiate their way into this new adolescent arena, learning the social codes as they carve out a sense of shared identity within new groups. Neither the expectations of the official roles nor those of less official roles are clearly defined or understood by the early adolescent as he or she enters a new social space.

This creates a critical period as early adolescents attempt to define and display appropriate conduct. In this transitional period, what may be regarded as appropriate behavior is unclear. Near the end of the year, Tiffany's parents described her transition into adolescence in this way:

LARRY SCHMIDT: I think it's okay to bend the rules, but not to break them. As a father I've watched these girls try to figure that out this year. It's okay to go seven miles over the speed limit, but not eight. What Tiffany's doing this year is figuring out what those new limits are. In sixth grade, they know the rules. They know the limits. They know the structure and the boundaries. But in seventh grade, they are expecting more freedom, and they are more angry when someone pushes them and says "You stepped over the boundaries" because their assumption is that, "Hey, I'm responsible. I'm free to make my own decisions." So when Tiffany was disciplined or got in trouble as a sixth grader, she knew she was stepping over the boundaries. She knew that she was going to get in trouble. In seventh grade, she had to refigure what those boundaries were, and what is seven miles over the speed limit rather than eight miles over the speed limit.

KAREN SCHMIDT: I want her to be a strong woman. And I know she's boisterous, but I don't think that is really a roadblock for her. I think that's important for her because nobody's going to step on her. Nobody is going to hold her back. She's gonna set the limits not somebody else.

Using metaphors of speed limits, roadblocks, and boundaries, Tiffany's parents articulate their understanding of their daughter's transition into adolescence. As a junior high teacher, I had felt those tensions of testing limits and bumping up against boundaries.

Suspended between childhood and adulthood, seventh graders must negotiate new rules and rituals, learn new ways of being in the world of school and home. Lauren explained, "They [teachers] expect us to be good all the time, but we are teenagers now." As newcomers to the junior high, these girls had limited ways to assert identity or proclaim power. I would argue that a new independence is afforded to adolescent females through literacy. Literacy provided a tangible means by which to claim status, challenge authority, and document social allegiances. Note-passing and writing on the rest-room walls, for example, served as acts of resistance while also creating strong bonds of solidarity among the girls.

Over the course of the year, the girls turned to literacy to assist them in defining and displaying their more adult roles. Angie, for example, described her reason for reading teen magazines in this way: "They tell you about woman stuff." Tiffany agreed, "See, it [*Sassy* magazine] shows you what's cool, and what's it's like to be a teenager today." Through literacy, just as Christian-Smith (1993) argues, the girls "construct and reconstruct their desires and gender subjectivities, as well as their awareness of social differences and power relations" (pp. 1–2).

Through these pages, I offer a window into the lived experience of two sets of best friends going about their daily routines at home and at school. In what follows, I discuss how (1) students embrace and resist particular social roles; (2) participation in classrooms is influenced by the underlife present within the school; (3) one's membership within groups regulates literate practices; and (4) social roles are defined and constrained by texts.

I attempt to make visible the vast tangle of competing expectations and allegiances that shape classroom contexts. Throughout the year, the girls' performances challenge the notion that effective literacy classrooms can be built on personal response and free choice. The girls, constrained by their social roles, coopted literate practices when forced to work with those outside their circle of significance; yet they maintained the appearance of performing in socially sanctioned ways. Commentaries on their class performances sounded remarkably like finessing intricate maneuvers on some sophisticated board game; they carefully calculated to guard against disclosure or alignment with those judged beneath them in the social hierarchy. Within the classroom setting, the girls all used literacy to present a particular kind of self. Literate practices could make invisible social roles and allegiances visible. Group members constructed their literate practices in direct opposition to other groups they considered to be childish. Cleo reported, "I don't read what they [Angie and Tiffany] read." Lauren remarked: "What do they [Cleo and Dottie] read? They probably just read books. They have nothing better to do."

The discourse currently circulating around student-centered pedagogy denies the power of the peer dynamic. Students' performances within the classroom cannot be free from sociopolitical tangles. "Free choices" are not free from the webs of social relationships. Students' selections are tied to their social relationships and filtered through their cultural assumptions of appropriate social roles. Since learning is enmeshed in social webs, I argue that a student-centered curriculum must consider the tangles that constrict students' performances. The girls candidly articulated such constrictions. Dottie explained, "It's like last year, I could sometimes kinda say more. When you're in junior high, everything's different."

NOTE

1. All names given for the school district, teachers, and students are fictitious.

CHAPTER 1

"When You're in Junior High, Everything's Different"

Firmly rooted within the rural Midwest, Northern Hills Community School District draws its student population from two counties, from farms and tiny towns that dot the rolling patchwork of corn, soybean, and alfalfa fields, quilted together with road and river and grove. The district lines wrap around a metropolitan area and carve off the northern and eastern edges, leaving the urban center for a neighboring district to the west. Often the winds bring to campus the smell of roasting cereal from the grain factory located in the nearby urban center.

NORTHERN HILLS COMMUNITY SCHOOL DISTRICT

Situated at the northern edge of one small town, surrounded on three sides by farm land, the upper elementary, junior high, and senior high school buildings share a sprawling central campus. This configuration makes the Educational Service Center, baseball diamonds, track, football fields, and high school auditorium easily accessible to all. Twice a day, double rows of yellow school buses line the parking lot that separates the upper elementary school from the junior/senior high school. Twice a day, students scramble past Oak Creek, a new housing development where many professional families dwell in spacious two- and three-story homes built away from the city to ensure a safe and secure neighborhood. Commuting to work in the nearby urban area, professionals often move here to enroll their children in a school district endorsed as a center of excellence by the governor.

Recognized by school personnel throughout the state as one of its finest educational institutions, Northern Hills is often perceived as serving a homogeneous population, almost exclusively Euro-American and quite affluent. While this perception holds some truth, a close examina-

6

tion reveals more subtle differences than at first apparent. It is true that a 1991–1992 demographic study of student population identifies nearly 97% of the population as Euro-American, but many students live in homes that look very different from those just across the street in the luxurious Oak Park Division. Straddling boundaries, the district buses students from less visible and less affluent city apartment buildings, trailer parks, and farms.

The junior high principal reported the socioeconomic status of the families of the student population in the following manner: 70% professional, 15% working class, and 15% trailer parks. Such statistics of socioeconomic status which distinguish working class from trailer park make visible an underlying assumption about families who live in trailer parks. The principal's distinction between working class and trailer parks echoes what I heard repeatedly in private conversations in many midwestern communities and schools, conversations in which judgments about a child's residence equate higher socioeconomic status with language-rich homes and caring parents (Finders & Lewis, 1993, 1994).

Such judgments disappear when one reads school and community literature. "Part of the Pride," the district's slogan, circulates on handbooks and letterheads, promoting the keen sense of accomplishment that pervades the conversations of community leaders, school officials, and faculty members. Northern Hills prides itself on keeping abreast of the latest national pedagogical and assessment strategies. The district employs four full-time curriculum coordinators who prepare materials and provide in-service education for its staff. There is little turnover in faculty positions here, where the elementary teaching load is 20–25 students and the secondary teaching load is generally kept between 100 and 110 students.

At Parkview Elementary, Northern Hills Community Schools brings together from its three lower elementary buildings all 500 fifth and sixth graders. Students at Parkview remain in self-contained homerooms. Individual homerooms function as traditional self-contained elementary classrooms, with daily literacy instruction in language arts and literature. Each homeroom is joined by two more to form "teams." Teams are housed close together and cooperate for large-group presentations, field trips, and theater performances. Students remain together for all content instruction except reading, which is ability-grouped within each team.

The junior high is separated from Parkview by only a parking lot, yet the division represents a much greater distance than the three-minute walk it involves. Sixth graders at Parkview, the oldest students in the building, are often rewarded with special privileges such as running errands, serving as library assistants, patrolling playgrounds, and monitoring hallways. Seventh grade marks the beginning of the junior high experience. At Northern Hills, seventh graders are the newcomers to the junior high, a brown brick structure with a split foyer built in the 1960s that houses all 531 seventh and eighth graders. Here, seventh graders are just learning the rules and rituals that accompany junior high life. They have lost their senior status to eighth graders, who hold the leadership positions in student government, athletic clubs, and all extracurricular activities.

The structure and schedule of the junior high divide each day into seven discrete segments in which students receive daily instruction in math, science, social studies, and language arts, with an alternating schedule provided for instruction in music, art, and physical education. An exploratory strand is added at the junior high level with six weeks of instruction in each of the following areas: foreign language, home economics, and industrial arts. Also, at the junior high the following extracurricular activities become available: one-act plays, band, orchestra, vocal music, volleyball, tennis, football, basketball, wrestling, and track. In traveling from room to room, interacting with a different set of classmates for each subject, meeting with seven different teachers with different rules and expectations, seventh graders encounter unfamiliar tensions and obstacles.

A colorful mural cloaks the entrance hallway of the junior high building, portraying the rich and rolling countryside. There among the motley green fields, ready to greet all who enter, are the school's mascot—a lion—and the school's slogan—"Part of the Pride." This sense of belonging and pride permeates the atmosphere at the school where, by virtue of enrollment, students are considered to be adolescents.

SOCIOCULTURAL PERSPECTIVES ON LITERACY

"Literacy" has historically referred to the acts of reading and writing and the cognitive consequences of such acts (Goody & Watt, 1963; Olson, 1977). A sociocultural view of literacy regards literacy as socially based and culturally specific. Since language is a social event, communications can be understood and explained only within their connections to a concrete situation (Heath, 1983; Scribner & Cole, 1981). According to Vygotsky (1962), all utterances take place within a social situation: There is no such thing as an isolated speaker or text. Speech mediates thought, which is a product of social interrelationships, a dialectic between self and community. Zebroski (1989) summarizes Vygotsky's key ideas in the following propositions: Self is social; self is created, constructed, composed; self is permeable, porous, fluid; self is dynamic and developing; self is semiotic; self is refined and developed through play. Wertsch (1991) extends the theories of Vygotsky by drawing on Bakhtin to develop a more comprehensive understanding of voice as dialogic. He argues that "human communication and psychological processes are characterized by a dialogicality of voices: When a speaker produces an utterance, at least two voices can be heard simultaneously" (p. 13). This extension of Vygotskian theory emphasizes the dynamism of every text and the situatedness of the speaker within cultural, historical, and institutional settings.

Within this sociocultural framework, definitions of literacy have expanded beyond simply the ability to read and write, or perhaps more precisely such ability is now seen as deeply enmeshed in wider circumstances. Because language is now understood as situated within specific social, cultural, and historical settings, a reconception of literacy as necessarily plural emerges in current literature (e.g., Dyson & Freedman, 1990; Gee, 1990; Szwed, 1981). A review of this changing conception of literacy is documented by Dyson and Freedman (1990) and Freedman, Dyson, Flower, and Chafe (1987).

Dyson (1992) explains that when people speak or write, they are engaging in a dialogue socially situated within multiple relations of power "and they do so with a sense of the social and power relationships implicit in those dialogues" (p. 4). Understanding the link between language and power makes visible sociopolitical tensions that create and constrain social roles.

Drawing extensively from Erving Goffman (1959, 1961), I define social roles as attached to a given status in a given context, as the enactment of rights and duties attached to a given status (Goffman, 1959, p. 16). Goffman defines social interactions as performances enacted for particular audiences. In other words, social roles shift depending on who is present and what the established expectations are of those present. I am not suggesting that social roles are put on like outer garments to protect or to conceal a true self, but rather that roles represent multiple and shifting selves. Defining a social role not as static but as a performative act allows one to examine critically the context and the roles that are made available therein. Brooke (1991) explains, "Each context holds certain expectations for how individuals will act and evaluates the worth of individuals in relations to these expectations" (p. 19).

Goffman (1959) distinguishes between center stage and backstage regions, which he characterizes in the following manner:

> Here costumes and other parts of personal front may be adjusted and scruti-
> nized for flaws. Here the team can run through its performance, checking
> for offending expressions when no audience is present to be affronted by
> them; here poor members of the team, who are expressively inept, can be
> schooled or dropped from the performance. (p. 112)

According to anthropologist James Scott (1990), the only way to
examine issues of power is to assess the discrepancy between the hidden transcripts defined as "discourse that takes place 'offstage,' beyond
direct observation by powerholders," and the public transcripts defined
as "the open interaction between subordinates and those who dominate" (pp. 4–5). At present, much important scholarship has provided
a clearer understanding of the patterns of classroom discourse, or in
Scott's terms, "the public transcripts" (see, e.g., Cazden, 1988). Yet,
more studies are needed that examine the offstage regions, with consideration of how hidden transcripts might disrupt the public.

If we accept a construction of text as socially situated within multiple
relations of power and further accept self as constructed by the rules
and rituals of the community, then literacy events, ordered and organized by societal norms, must be understood as an integral part of this
socialization process. Throughout this study, I maintain a focus on the
literacy event as defined by Heath (1982):

> A conceptual tool useful in examining within particular communities of
> modern society the actual forms and functions of oral and literate traditions
> and co-existing relationships between spoken and written language. A liter-
> acy event is any occasion in which a piece of writing is integral to the nature
> of participants' interactions and their interpretive processes. (p. 93)

Britton (1970) refers to language as a representation, as "a verbally
organized world schema" (p. 28), a map used for guidance from one
experience to the next. Literacy, then, can provide a window onto the
complex processes at work as individuals move from one context to
another.

Against a sociocultural backdrop, "literacy" as it is used throughout
this study retains the traditional definition and will refer exclusively to
print sources. By adhering to a traditional marker of educational success, this study can examine issues that currently circulate around literacy learning by documenting literacy in use. A focus on the rich variety
of print sources available in different contexts can make visible competing influences and conflicting perceptions that focal students must negotiate in order to fully participate in each context. Literacy and the
mesh of lives, classrooms, and relationships in which they are embed-

ded serve as a window onto the processes in operation as adolescents begin to negotiate adult roles, roles that change across institutional and social settings.

ADOLESCENT GIRLS: SHIFTING CONCEPTIONS

The boundaries of adolescence are marked by social and physical changes (Klein, 1990). In this country, with the publication of his 1904 two-volume set *Adolescence*, G. Stanley Hall became known as the father of adolescence. Hall conceptualized the period of adolescence as biologically determined, with little consideration for any social or cultural influences (Santrock, 1993, p. 13). Hall's view of adolescence as a period of "storm and stress" characterized as "a turbulent time charged with conflict and mood swings" (Santrock, 1993, p. 14) persists, with hormonal factors often accounting for the marked fluctuations in adolescent behaviors (Brooks-Gunn & Reiter, 1990, p. 43). Early research conducted by Anna Freud and Erik Erikson insisted that a "lack of stress during adolescence was a sign of abnormality and hence a cause for concern" (quoted in Apter, 1990, p. 70).

Coleman's (1961) landmark study grew out of this storm-and-stress model and led to a construction of adolescence as a subculture sharply distinct from adult culture. Brown (1990) writes of Coleman's monolithic adolescent peer culture:

> In Coleman's data and conclusions three factors sharply differentiated the adolescent peer culture from adult society. First, adolescents' career aspirations reflected youthful hedonism rather than a concern with making substantive contributions to society. . . . Second, criteria for popularity with peers devalued academic achievement in favor of characteristics less valuable in the eyes of adults, such as athletic prowess or membership in the "leading crowd." Third, parents and children seemed to espouse opposite views on such issues as the most desirable characteristics of a friend or dating partner. Coleman concluded that adolescent peer culture drew teenagers into a preoccupation with the present and therefore, alienated them from adult society. (p. 173)

Along with the storm and stress that characterize this developmental period, other attributes include the increasing importance of peer groups and the detachment from significant adults (Brooks-Gunn & Reiter, 1990; Brown, 1990; Feldman & Elliott, 1990).

Past studies that explore the lived experiences of adolescents have relied on male participants (Eckert, 1989; Everhart, 1983; Foley, 1990;

MacLeod, 1987; Willis, 1977). Females are missing from conversations of adolescence (see two important exceptions in Shuman, 1986, for research with junior high girls; and Griffin, 1985, for research on females' movement from adolescence into the work place).

Assumptions of adolescence as a life stage are now beginning to shift toward a conception of adolescence as socially situated rather than biologically driven. Recent research problematizes many commonly held assumptions about adolescence (e.g., Apter, 1990; Feldman & Elliott, 1990; Takanishi, 1993). Apter (1990) and Comer (1993) argue for the necessity of maintaining close ties among children and adults during this period. Fine and Macpherson (1993) criticize studies of adolescence because often they do not take into account marked differences in terms of race, class, gender, or sexual orientation.

Along with many feminist scholars (Britzman, 1993; Davies, 1989; Fine & Macpherson, 1993; hooks, 1990), Biklen and Pollard (1993) describe gender as the social construction of sex: "What we have come to identify as belonging to men's or women's behaviors, attitudes, presentation of self, and so on is produced by social relationships and continually negotiated and maintained within cultures" (p. 2). Britzman explains, "Social constructivists argue against the view that identities are stable, natural, or unique. Individuals, they argue, are not the sole authors of the self but rather are authored in language and by social practice" (p. 32). In other words, girls' roles are neither biologically determined nor individually constructed. Various expectations of society socialize young girls into particular gendered roles.

Carol Gilligan and her colleagues (Gilligan, Lyons, & Hanmer, 1990; Gilligan, Ward, & Taylor, 1988) confront the issue of gender roles and argue that the hierarchical structure of schools works against girls, who are more inclined to use language to connect rather that compete. It is important to note that Gilligan's work is based on self-reports that provide important insights into how girls perceive their roles and relationships. While such methodology documents sets of beliefs, it does not examine how girls might actually negotiate such sets of beliefs. Gender studies must address how behaviors are socially ordered and controlled. Furthermore, studies that investigate adolescent culture must acknowledge gender differences within the expectations, rules, and rituals that inform daily routines.

In cross-cultural anthropological studies, Schlegel and Barry (1991) define social adolescence as the period between puberty and the full assumption of adult roles. They write of gender differences:

> In the United States, for example, there may be considerable variation among ethnic groups and social classes. In the middle and upper classes

where child labor is not needed at home or in family enterprises, adolescents of both sexes are likely to spend a good deal of time with their agemates, and the difference between boys and girls may be less marked. In working-class households or in families of Hispanic or of recent Middle Eastern or Asian extraction, girls may be expected to spend their afterschool hours at home while boys may be away from home, working or at leisure with their peers. (p. 43)

Clearly, gender roles entangle with other dimensions of the social world, dimensions often denied in the school context. (See, for example, documentation of schools' inattentiveness to social-class differences in the work of Brantlinger, 1993, and Lareau, 1987). Like Brantlinger and Lareau, Willis (1977), MacLeod (1987), and Eckert (1989) also focus on issues of social class in their research. While their studies focus on adolescent boys, they make claims similar to Gilligan's about the structuring of school, suggesting that school failure for working-class teens may be based on the fact that the only available roles for these young people are those of victim or rebel. Available roles for girls are often presented in a similar dichotomy: good girls and bad girls (Fine & Macpherson, 1993), selfish or selfless (Gilligan, 1982).

While there are marked differences in adolescence across cultures, Schlegel and Barry (1991) note nearly universal differential treatment of girls and boys in preparation for social roles and more marked divisions between the sexes at the time of adolescence. They write of this period:

Along with training for specific roles, there is learning in the sense of cognitive and affective reorganization away from the behavioral modes of childhood and toward adult modes. The child is characterized by dependency, subordination, and social asexuality, even as these vary across cultures. As *his* social scope, responsibilities and expectations enlarge, the adolescent assumes greater autonomy, more of a peer relationship with same-sex adults, and an interest in sexual activities. Such unlearning and relearning is unlikely to be without cost to the adolescents or to their families, who must also undergo changes in the ways they respond to their maturing children. (p. 8) [Emphasis added]

Entry into junior high presents a critical juncture of such necessary *unlearning* and *relearning*. Adults and adolescents must all renegotiate their roles and relationships—roles and relationships informed not simply by entry into adolescence but also by how adolescence is socially situated within multiple cultural, historical, and institutional settings.

The dynamics of early adolescence present a critical juncture in social and cognitive development. A greater emphasis on academics, an increase in expectations for social experiences outside the home, and an intensification of differential gender roles position early adolescents at a pivotal juncture in their lives. It is within these multiple processes of renegotiating values and behaviors that particular roles become available to adolescents, roles informed by race, class, and gender. Building on research on gender, socioeconomic class, and literacy, this study carves out how early adolescent girls use literacy in multiple contexts and, in turn, examines how social roles are shaped and mediated by diverse literate practices.

In summary, it is this complex weave, knotty and coarse as it may be, in which adolescents construct their identities. Too much of the literature of adolescence points to fixed stages and prescribed scripts into which adolescents must squeeze their lives rather than to a focus on mediated action and agency as means to stretch the fabric of which lives are woven. Concerns for how rules and rituals, expectations and actions, within and between contexts might change at childhood's end have seldom been documented. In one breath, a student lunges forward with, "Hey, don't treat me like a baby. I can do this myself," and in the next, recoils with "How do you expect me to do this? I'm just a kid." Adults offer promises of independence and retract such offers, often in fear for their child's safety. It is as if moments in this dynamic are held in suspension by a tangled web of conflicting expectations, assumptions, aspirations, and allegiances.

"JUST REGULAR GIRLS": PRESENTING SOCIAL ROLES

A few students looked up when I entered Mr. Stone's sixth-grade classroom for the first time. From his desk, Mr. Stone introduced me as someone from the university who was interested in learning about their reading and writing practices. Students seemed unimpressed and returned to their reading selections. Neither the buzz from the fans nor the hot May breeze rustling papers distracted these students from their reading. I moved to the back of the room and slid into an empty seat near Mr. Stone's desk.

The desks were pushed together and clustered into sections. Near the front on the left-hand side, four girls sat together, each reading a novel: Three were reading novels from the Babysitters' Club series, one was reading *Goose Bumps* by R. L. Stine. Across from them were two groups of boys, reading a little more loudly from *Sports Illustrated*, a local newspaper, *Beckett's Guide to Baseball Card Collection*, and *The Guinness Book of World Records*. One of the "techno trio," as Mr. Stone called them, was reading a science fiction fantasy novel, the second sat engrossed in a computer reference guide, and the third flipped through the pages of his own computer-made comic book. Behind the first group of boys sat a cluster of three girls. One girl was reading *Anne of Green Gables*, another *Otherwise Known as Sheila the Great*, and a third *The Adventures of Tom Sawyer*.

Mr. Stone whispered to me, pointing out the four clusters of students:

FIGURE 1.1. Mr. Stone's sixth-grade classroom.

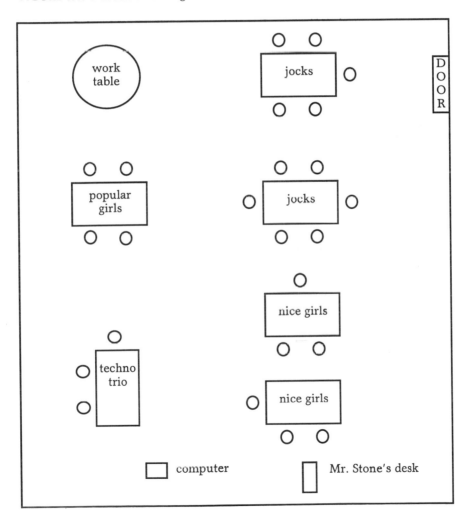

They're my jocks—you know, the athletic kids. Those girls are the popular group. Those others are the nicest girls you could ever work with—every teacher's dream students. Actually they're all good girls. And the techno trio's over there. I had to put tape on the floor to keep them from moving all over the place. [See Figure 1.1]

He smiled and continued, explaining that by this time of year he allowed students to self-select their seating arrangement, "as long as they can handle it." He explained that students needed to make more decisions as they prepared for the move to junior high:

I want them to learn to make their own decisions and then accept the consequences of that, and they really don't have much trouble sitting by their friends. They know by now what I expect during S.S.R. [Sustained Silent Reading]. They read and I read. Sure the boys get a little noisy at times. The girls may giggle. But see. They are all reading.

Indeed they were. Mr. Stone returned to his copy of *Sports Illustrated*, and I returned to my observations.

Mr. Stone was the first to distinguish between the two groups of girlfriends that he observed in his classroom: "the nice girls" (those who in his eyes appeared quiet and complacent) and "the popular girls" (those who were outgoing and participated in many school-sponsored functions). Teachers, administrators, and the girls themselves charted separate and clearly bounded friendship groups. The seating arrangement in Mr. Stone's room illustrates the friendship circles present in his sixth-grade classroom.

Since research on adolescence suggests that peer-group relations become more salient as they are distanced from adult supervision (Brooks-Gunn & Reiter, 1990; Brown, 1990; Feldman & Elliott, 1990), membership in one of two distinct networks of friends was the main criterion for selection of focal students. I followed Angie, Lauren, and Tiffany (self-reported best friends from the popular girls) and Cleo and Dottie (best friends from the nice girls) and their larger circle of girl-friends from May of their sixth-grade year through the completion of seventh grade, documenting their reading and writing practices at home and at school.

Girls were selected as focal students for three reasons. First, from a feminist perspective, it has been argued that a female's sense of self is often organized around being able to make and then maintain affiliations and relationships (Belenky, Clinchy, Goldberger, & Tarule, 1986; Gilligan, 1988; Gilligan, Lyons, & Hanmer, 1990). Literacy events in and out of school provide an arena in which the individual girl learns to read and write her roles and relationships; yet, the dynamics of such relationships have been largely under-researched. Second, both school structure and popular adolescent literature have been criticized because they seem to constrict the roles available to young women (Apple, 1986; Gilligan, 1988; Stretch, 1991). This study examines from the perspectives of the girls themselves how such literature is received and how the structure of the school impacts on them. Third, as a woman, I had greater access to social and private functions of young women.

By meeting with focal students informally outside the school context, I gained their trust slowly and negotiated a relationship that did not fit their established patterns with significant adults. Dottie came to know that I would keep her embarrassing secret that her parents' car had been repossessed, and she couldn't miss the school bus home for any reason. Cleo began sharing her feminist essays and poetry with me, trusting that I would not tell her teacher about them. Tiffany and Angie soon began handing over notes deemed "too obscene" for their mothers or teachers. In October, I overheard Tiffany announcing, "That's not a teacher, that's Peg." After a period of testing, she felt confident that I did not embrace the adult role in the school context—in other words, I would not report her misconduct to the principal's office.

As sixth and seventh graders, the focal students had limited access to social outings outside the school context, and I occasionally drove them to the mall or out for a pizza or hamburgers. This allowed me the opportunity not only to observe them in induced natural contexts but to negotiate a relationship with them that did not position me as an authority figure. Early on, there were moments in which I was tested by focal students. On several occasions, a girl would not allow me to see a note that she thought inappropriate for adults. I did not report such practices as writing on a rest-room wall or faking illness to avoid an exam. I avoided conveying any negative judgment, and as the study progressed, I slowly gained their trust and was permitted to receive writing deemed "too gross" or "too revealing" for parents or teachers. As the year progressed, focal students began to see their roles as my teacher and wanted me to understand what being a teenager was really like. So that I would, as they said, "get it right," I was soon being invited to their homes, slumber parties, and dances.

After one year of documenting the literate lives of two circles of girlfriends, I struggled to represent them. As I had on numerous occasions, I turned to the expertise of each group.

M.F.: When I write about you, what do you want me to say? How should I describe who you are?

TIFFANY: Um. Say we're just girls.
LAUREN: Yeah, just regular girls.
ANGIE: Not Woof-Woofs.
TIFFANY: Not babies. Just regular girls.

In a separate interview, the other circle of friends had this to say about themselves:

DOTTIE: I don't know. We're girls, just girls.
CLEO: Not like those other girls.
DOTTIE: Not like those popular air-heads.
CLEO: Just regular girls. Real girls.

As active agents, the girls construct their own history, but, of course, a normalizing discourse is internalized from the larger culture. Certain regularities impose a kind of script on these early adolescents as they set out on a sociosexual journey toward adulthood. What does it mean from the perspective of these early adolescent females to be a "regular girl"? How is such a role enacted? Throughout this book, I will share the girls' perspectives on what roles are available and how those roles are negotiated in multiple contexts.

Adolescence is at times referred to as a "culture" because of its marked distinctions from adult life. The metaphor of culture works only if we acknowledge an interanimation of values, beliefs, and discursive practices diffusing through permeable boundaries within and across communities. Cintron (1991) problematizes the notion of any community identity. He writes:

> As Bakhtin (1981) suggests, communities that are in contact interanimate each other. They infect, disrupt, and even discharge their differences during their interaction such that each community's beliefs, values, and language system (including its way of speaking) are exchanged, resulting in ephemeral identities. (p. 24)

Adolescents move among multiple and often competing rules and rituals of different contexts. This study explores the "cultures" that adolescent girls perceive and construct through their literate practices.

It may be assumed that a girl's "rite of passage" bursts into her life biologically; hence no outward "rite" has to be performed. But in this society, physical maturation is not accepted as a sign of adulthood for males or females, so the need exists for other forms of recognition of "passage." Literacy serves such a need, marking the passage. Girls use literacy to control, moderate, and measure their growth into adulthood. I would argue that a new independence is afforded to adolescent females through literacy. It might be argued further that the recognition of their literacies (often in such marked events as receiving a high school diploma) signifies a reintegration into society and their acceptance as adults by adults. In other words, literacies served as a visible rite of passage, as a cultural practice to mark oneself as in control, as powerful.

Follow, if you will, as relationships unfold in the following notes dug out from under the mattresses of 12-year-old girls, just three of the hundreds of notes that I collected over the past year. Embedded within the contents of these notes is a set of cultural values and gendered norms. Such notes, it seems, serve to acculturate early adolescents to particular social roles.

> Tiffany,
> Hi! What's ↑? N.M.H.[Not Much Here] I am in social studies right now and I am in the front row. IT IS BORING. I am in a wild mood now. I hope I can do something this weekend. Will you talk to you know who for me? S.O.S. [Sorry sO Sloppy or Sweet Or Sexy]
>> B.F.F. [Best Friends Forever] Angie

> Lauren, What's up? N.M.H. [Not Much Here] I'm in science and it's SOOOO boring! Aaron says hi! Really who do you think I should go with? I like Jacob Walton. Do you think he will go with me? Don't show this to anyone!
>> Yo Sara

> Lauren, What's up? You have to find me a boyfriend. I'm sick of being single for over a month. Please find somebody that you think likes me and ask him out. (But check with me first to see if I like him also.) I prefer eighth graders. Please Help!
>> Bye! B.B.F. [Best Buds Forever]
>> Kate
> P.S. Can I go trick or treating with you if you can go?
> P.M.S. I'm so desperate for a boyfriend!

Notice the juxtaposition of interests in the last note: from the child ("Can I go trick or treating with you if you can go?") and from the young woman ("I'm so desperate for a boyfriend"). The playfulness of the postscript does not diminish the sense of urgency that permeates this note.

Just as these notes might appear childish or foolish, literate behaviors in a seventh-grade classroom might also appear chaotic or inappropriate to anyone who hasn't spent time there. Yet, emerging identities and strong allegiances give shape to these literate behaviors. Likewise, hidden within these seemingly chaotic states are the rules and rituals that govern and give order to such behaviors and make particular social roles available to these early adolescents.

Over the period of one year, a host of performances was revealed. Yet clearly all roles were exclusive and often appeared to be scripted. Throughout the year, these girls insisted that they were just regular girls. They most often defined themselves by making sharp contrasts between their group of girlfriends and others: "Not Woof-Woofs," "Not like those popular air-heads." Divisions between groups appear negatively charged through the lenses of the girls themselves, who insisted that they and their friends were "just girls" but cast multiple derogatory labels on those outside their friendship networks. The "popular girls" were often whispered about by other girls who referred to them as "the snots," "the snobs," and "the richy-rich." Based on their failure to meet fashion or beauty standards, the "nice girls" were literally barked at and called "dogs" and "woof-woofs" by girls outside their friendship circle. The girls were always quick to point out differences between groups, to make it clearly understood that they were not like "those other girls." I have chosen to refer to each group of girls as their mothers have:

> She is a much more social person than she was two or three years ago. With sports and friends and all. That's what's most important to her. She's really a *social queen*. [Tiffany's mother]

> Even when she was in kindergarten, she would get herself to school and then come home and help with dinner. I work nights, so she had to get up and get herself ready for school. I'm not going to be there all the time. . . . She's gotta do it. She's strong. She can take care of herself. She's a *tough cookie*. [Cleo's mother]

Already one can detect tension. Notice the apparent match between the ways in which one group of girls is viewed—by school personnel and parents—queens and popular girls; in contrast, the ways in which parents and school personnel view the other group is quite disparate—tough cookies and nice girls.

As illustrated in Figure 1.2, friendship circles were clearly bounded. At cafeteria tables, in the library, on the school grounds, invisible

FIGURE 1.2. Friendship circles.

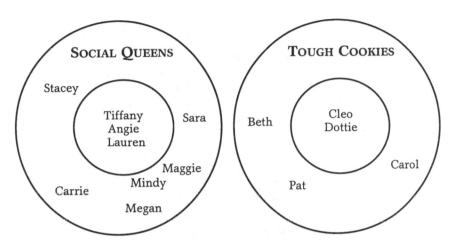

boundaries kept the focal students divided into two distinct social groups. Their literate practices were clearly bounded as well. As the study unfolded, it became increasingly clear that literate practices served to mark social boundaries.

The Social Queens

Characterized by their teacher and peers as the most popular girls in the school, Tiffany and Angie were best friends from one circle of friends. "The social queens" was a very large network of friends. Between 10 and 16 girls counted themselves as members of this circle: Lauren, Tiffany, and Angie made up one inner core. These three spent as much time together as their parents would allow.

Referring to each other as "best bud," Tiffany and Angie were rarely seen apart. Tiffany carried the nickname Big Red (given to her by Lauren, her other best friend) because of her large stature and bright red hair. On any given day, either girl confided that she hated the other one. On any given day, either girl claimed Lauren as her "best bud," leaving the other outside the inner circle, if only momentarily.

Tiffany, the youngest of five children, lived in town with her mother, brother, and stepfather. Her mother recently began college, training to become a registered nurse, and her stepfather worked for a large car dealership in the city. Tiffany was very well liked by her peers.

Her parents and teachers on occasion worried that her school work might suffer because of her "very outgoing nature."

Angie and her mother were active members of 4-H; however, Angie was also involved in piano, dance, dog shows, and photography. Her teachers perceived her as an outstanding student. She lived just outside of town on a farm with her mother, father, and younger brother and sister. Her mother was a teacher's assistant at a local elementary school. Her father farmed the land he inherited from his father and also worked at a factory in the city.

While I selected Tiffany and Angie as focal students, Lauren selected me. She was always first to greet me at school and repeatedly set up interviews with me. While I did not visit in her home, I observed and interviewed Lauren regularly. She was most often the center of any loud cluster of students. This seems consistent with her sixth-grade teacher's description of her: "Lauren's the straw that stirs the drink." Lauren participated in basketball, volleyball, and weight-lifting. She lived with her mother, older brother, and stepfather, and took great pride in "Sweetie Pies," her mother's successful home bakery business.

Angie and Tiffany spent most of their free time together, "conning" Angie's mom into driving them to games, dances, social events, or "just cruisin'." Sleepovers most regularly occurred at Angie's farm because, as the girls all reported, "She's got the coolest place to hang," and because they all looked to Angie's mother for advice, comfort, and transportation.

The Tough Cookies

Cleo and Dottie were self-reported best friends from another circle. As described by their sixth-grade teacher, "the nicest girls, every teacher's ideal students," they were a group made up of five friends: Beth, Pat, Carol, Cleo, and Dottie.

Cleo lived with her mother, father, younger brother, and sister on the eastern edge of town in a large trailer park. Her mother worked at the grain factory in the city as she had for the past 10 years, and at the beginning of this study, Cleo's father had just become employed with a trucking firm. Cleo had been identified as gifted by the school standards and participated in the Extended Learning Program (ELP). Teachers generally perceived Cleo's socioeconomic background to be lower than that of most of her classmates. Her sixth-grade teacher said, "She's a super girl. She doesn't have nice clothes, but she has very good self-esteem. She's strong. Cleo is not afraid to stand up for her rights. She doesn't care who they are. They can be the richest kid. It doesn't bother her any." Cleo said of herself, "I wish I could change the way people view me."

Dottie lived with her younger sister, mom, and stepdad in a trailer park across a four-lane highway from Cleo's home. At the beginning of this study, neither parent was employed. They received public assistance and financial support from extended family members. As the study progressed, Dottie's stepfather became employed. Dottie's teacher described her in this way: "She's a perfectionist. Dottie is so concerned about school success that she calls her teachers at home regularly to make sure she is on the right track." Her sixth-grade teacher said, "She's quiet and conscientious. She wants to do well. This year she has gotten close to Cleo and that helps her confidence."

Cleo, Dottie, and their friends ate lunch together at school but spent little of their out-of-school time together. On weekends they each spent most of their leisure time at home with their families. Dottie and Cleo both expressed regularly how much they enjoyed and needed time alone, away from both friends and family.

Although each friendship group was quite willing to cast those outside their circle in stereotypic roles, they were overtly aware of multiple and competing roles for themselves. In a private interview, Cleo described herself in this way: "It's almost like there are multiple people, like there are multiple me's, and this is the one that goes to school, and this is what other people expect." Cleo's articulation of "multiple me's" reveals an overt awareness of multiple and shifting selves. Similarly, Lauren was aware of competing expectations. She explained, "They [teachers] expect us to be good all the time, but we are teenagers now." What other people expected—teachers, parents, and peers—greatly shaped the attitudes and actions of each focal student.

Within two distinct circles of friends, the girls used literacy as a powerful tool to make allegiances visible, to construct boundaries around friendship circles. Literacy was a means of self-presentation. Identification with and division from friendship circles might be accomplished by carrying a particular book or folding a note in a particular manner. Likewise, the girls used literacy to control, moderate, and measure their growth into adulthood.

As the study unfolded, I became increasingly aware of the girls' conscious efforts to enact particular roles. They used literate practices to present a particular kind of self. Seeing roles and relationships in print documented one's social position. Literacy was of central importance, serving as a written record, fixing roles and relationships in print. From the first day I met the students of Northern Hills, I observed that their literate choices were clearly declarations of cultural masculine and feminine identification. For the most part boys chose to read newspapers, sports books, and sports magazines. Competition was central to their presentation of self. In contrast, girls selected novels. Girls embraced a social role that privileged relationships. As 12- and 13-year-olds, these girls had limited ways with which to assert identity or seek power. Literacy proved a tangible means by which to document their social allegiances, claim status, and challenge authority. In a world that was for the most part out of their control, early adolescent girls turned to literacy as a tangible form of power.

OFFICIAL EXPECTATIONS AND LITERATE UNDERLIFE

Within the school, students must conform to a set of official expectations, yet, as Goffman (1961) explains:

> Whenever we look at a social establishment, we find a counter to this first theme; we find that participants decline in some way to accept the official view of what they should be putting into and getting out of the organization and, behind this, of what sort of self and world they are to accept for themselves. Where enthusiasm is expected, there will be apathy; where loyalty, there will be disaffection; where attendance, absenteeism; where robustness, some kind of illness; where deeds are to be done, varieties of inactivities. We find a multitude of homely little histories, each in its way a movement of liberty. Whenever worlds are laid on, underlives develop. (pp. 304–305)

During the year of data collection, I became aware of two literate systems in operation: sanctioned literacies (those literacies that are recognized, circulated, and sanctioned by adults in authority) and what I have come to refer to as "literate underlife" (those practices that refuse in some way to accept the official view, practices designed and enacted to challenge and disrupt the official expectations). Within the institution, the two systems operated simultaneously, demanding adherence to competing expectations, rules, and rituals.

Out of sight and out of control of those in authority, literate underlife created space for girls to secure social roles, to present a self less controlled by adults in authority. The need for literate underlife is perhaps greatest during early adolescence, a time when young people are breaking away from adult control, trying out new adult roles for themselves. Suspended between childhood and adulthood, the girls in this study turned to literate underlife to negotiate between competing sets of expectations. Literate underlife served, it seemed, two functions: providing play time away from adults and providing opportunity to try on and test out more adult roles.

Since the structure of the school day demands much wait time— waiting for tardy and dismissal bells, instruction, materials, or discussion turns—the girls used literacies to entertain themselves and avoid boredom. In all of their literate underlife, there existed a tremendous sense of play. Literate underlife served, it seemed, as a kind of middle-school substitute for recess, providing playtime away from adults and away from the institutional demands of schooling. The girls entertained each other, wrote jokes and puns, created signs, parodied adults, and designed symbols that carried multiple meanings. On rest-room stalls, for example, they drew hearts, upside down and widened to illustrate a women's posterior. Also, the queens used PMS as the most common postscript on notes. When I questioned them about the meaning of PMS as a postscript, the queens laughed at me and wondered how I, as a woman, would not know about premenstrual syndrome. Indeed, they were overtly aware of their play with adult roles, with being a group of women.

All of the cookies and queens were regarded as "good girls" by their teachers—girls, one teacher said, "You can always count on to help you out." Just as Mr. Stone noted that all of the girls in the study were good girls, when I discussed my selections of focal students with the building principal, he commented, "Well that's great. They're all good girls. They're all good girls." Cast into such a role, each of the focal students negotiated how far out of bounds she might go and remain in good standing at school and at home. There were times, of course, when social queens might be reprimanded for laughing too loudly or turning in "average work," and times when the tough cookies did not participate as fully as their teachers might have preferred. Yet, in general, teachers, parents, school administrators, and the girls themselves regarded all of the focal students as cooperative. In like manner, Walkerdine (1990) writes, "In a recent study an overwhelming number of girls of all ages gave descriptions of their ideal girls which included the terms 'nice, kind and helpful'" (p. 51). This notion of the ideal, Walkerdine argues, connects good performance with docility and positions girls in roles that privilege helpfulness as the highest level of attainment. The queens and the cookies for the most part maintained the appearance of embracing the role of the nice, kind, and helpful girl while turning to backstage regions to resist. Literate underlife provided an opportunity to counter those official expectations.

After documenting the literate practices of these girls for one year, I argue that literate underlife is central to the development of the early adolescent female. During this period, adult rhetoric about becoming an adolescent revolves around issues of freedom, independence, and responsibility, yet actual practices in the school context most often constrict time, movement, and talk. Because communication becomes so tightly monitored by adults during this period, talk goes underground to avoid surveillance by those in authority. Early adolescents create and appropriate messages away from adults and other peers. Underlife provides an opportunity for the girls to refute official expectations and negotiate social roles within other powerful circles.

I turn now to those official expectations as they are presented at Northern Hills Junior High School.

LANGUAGE ARTS AT NORTHERN HILLS JUNIOR HIGH SCHOOL

Five full-time teachers and one three-quarter-time teacher make up the language arts department. Each full-time position consists of five sections of language arts, one study hall, and one preparation period daily. All six language arts teachers share a planning period to allow for collaboration. During this planning period, the language arts teachers come together in their language arts office to exchange materials, plan projects, wrestle with concerns for students, share treats, and enjoy one another's company.

The language arts office, a large classroom converted into an office with seven desks pushed together in the middle, allows for ample face-to-face conversation. Here, within the clutter of teachers' lives, samples of last year's student projects, stacks of curricular materials, and piles of papers, a strong sense of collegial respect and camaraderie permeates the room. Teetering precariously atop file cabinets, book orders wait to be sorted and new children's books and adolescent fiction wait to be shared. Here, in this literate haven—perhaps the only backstage region for the language arts staff—teachers relax a bit, let down their guard, and struggle together to understand their students' successes and failures as well as their own. Discussions wander from Gary Paulsen to Danielle Steele, from fudge brownie recipes to family crises.

Teachers at Northern Hills discussed with me their junior high language arts curriculum using terms such as "workshops" and "writing process pedagogy." Teachers had participated in the summer state writing institute and attended district-wide whole language workshops; all subscribed to what they called a "student-centered" philosophy. There appeared to be a strong consensus concerning appropriate pedagogy for junior high students. Gaining fluency by writing in a risk-free environment and connecting reading and writing to one's personal background were commonly articulated as the foundation of the language arts pedagogy.

The unifying theme in all of this talk was a commitment to a teaching style in which students would feel comfortable and safe. Mr. Tibidioux explained, "We want them to feel comfortable with their writing and more importantly, comfortable with who they are." In the language arts office, I often heard references to safety in regard to sound pedagogical decision making: "safe community" and "safe environment." A poster in one doorway proclaimed the language arts wing a "Safe Space." Teachers agreed that students must feel, as one described it, "safe in order to take risks."

At the junior high, language arts classes were often designed as reading and writing workshops in which students developed topics and worked individually or in groups. During such times, students pursued topics of personal interest. Teachers cited Nancie Atwell (1987) as a key source of their pedagogy, and often turned to work by Graves (1983) and Romano (1987) for assistance. At other times, reading, writing, listening, and speaking were integrated around thematic units such as mythology, animal stories, and science fiction. Whenever such units were in progress, time was preserved within the class structure for ongoing personal reading and writing choices. Students were expected to self-select novels and writing topics and to monitor their reading and writing habits. In Mrs. Zmoleck's class, the first 10–15 minutes of each class period were allocated for reading workshop on Mondays and Tuesdays, and writing workshop on Wednesdays and Thursdays; on Fridays students chose between reading or writing. In Mr. Tibidioux's class, daily journal writing began each class session and Fridays were designated reading workshop days.

At the junior high, students kept a reading/writing folder, and it was assessed periodically by teachers. Within each folder, students were expected to record their progress for the reading and writing workshop. Some pieces of writing within the folder were graded individually, and others were assessed as part of the whole. The reading grade was based on the number of pages read and on assessment of student-selected reading projects.

The language arts department supported goals for their students as described by Mrs. Zmoleck, the departmental chairperson, in the following manner:

> Well, curriculum coordinators would probably gasp, but my main goal is number one that they leave my class with an appreciation for

themselves, [and] others and have been able to find some enjoyment in writing. And I think if they find some kind of enjoyment in
it then they will be able to improve. At least more easily, so I try and
use reading and writing and speaking activities to help build that
appreciation for themselves and for others, too. I think that's what
junior high is all about.

"WHAT JUNIOR HIGH IS ALL ABOUT": SOCIAL ROLES AND THE DISCOURSE OF ADOLESCENCE

"What junior high is all about" is entangled in a discourse of adolescence that saturates our culture. The assumptions that undergird the
developmental period known as adolescence directly and consciously
shape teaching practices and social roles at Northern Hills Junior High
School. In conversation with teachers, one can readily detect a familiar
construction of adolescence equally apparent in the literature of educational psychology, popular culture, and teacher training. In conversations with teachers, I heard such comments as, "raging hormones,"
"They need their space," "They don't want us to get too close," "You
know how adolescents are; they're just a bundle of hormones,"
"They're wired to go off," "Hormone hostages," and "They need to
find that line so they can step over it." Such discourse holds that (1)
adolescents sever ties with adults; (2) peer groups become increasingly
influential social networks; (3) resistance is a sign of normalcy for the
adolescent; and (4) romance and sexual drive govern interests and relationships.

Such assumptions guided curricular decisions and governed
teacher–student interaction patterns. For instance, Mr. Stone, a sixth-
grade teacher, made the transition to seventh-grade social studies while
this study was in progress, stating as his reason a desire to engage with
students "more academically." As his first year with seventh graders
progressed, he described his loss of connectedness to students and their
families. Likewise, the girls noted changes in Mr. Stone as a junior high
teacher. One commented, "He like changed to a totally new person."
The man they had admired and respected turned "meaner," they said.
"He acts like he doesn't even know me," Cleo told me. Dottie commented, "He's not as nice as he used to be. He never laughs. He
doesn't tell jokes. He doesn't call me Sunny [the nickname he gave her]
anymore." Based on his understanding of this stage of development,
Mr. Stone altered his classroom practices to match the needs of the
adolescent, and it was most often assumed that all adolescents need the

same things. The discourse of adolescence directed him to be less personal and, as he said, "more academic."

Operating from a set of assumptions about what it means to be a junior high teacher, Mr. Stone constrained the kinds of relationships that he had formed with sixth graders. While recent research regards close connections with significant adults as central to positive personal identity for teens (Comer, 1993; Eccles & Harold, 1993), junior high teachers often construct a role that is less personal and more guarded. Students reported, for example, that Mr. Stone told fewer stories about his family and himself and remained closer to the text in his teaching.

Debra Zmoleck also regarded the role of a junior high teacher as more socially distant than that of an elementary teacher. In a discussion on hiring a new junior high language arts faculty member, she voiced concerns for a candidate who had been an elementary school teacher:

> She may not be happy because she'll expect too much contact with the kids. Kids this age don't want teachers to know that much about them. Not even their parents. They want to be on their own. Elementary teachers get too close. She better not hug any of them.

Note her use of the phrase "too close." Again, the assumption that all adolescents seek distance from significant adults is accepted without question. Severing ties with adults and building stronger allegiances with same-age peers are, of course, characteristic of the discourse of adolescence, which has normalized one way of being adolescent in our culture.

This study, too, was designed based on a controlling assumption that peer groups would become more salient as they were distanced from adult supervision. A focal student's mother problematized this assumption with my first phone call to her home. When I contacted Cleo's mother explaining that my study would explore how peer groups influence the reading and writing practices of adolescent girls, she clearly articulated a construction of adolescence that conflicted with mine:

> Cleo is gonna blow your theory all to hell. She doesn't share with other girls. She shares with me. She doesn't share with other girls. She's independent. She takes care of herself.

Yet, my own discursive filters were so strong that it literally took months of documentation of counter-examples to refute the dominant image of the "normal" adolescent. During part of my year of data collection, the term "adolescence" created a screen that deflected attention away from viewing the complexities of the lived experiences of the focal students. I held tightly to my bedrock assumption about the growing significance of best friends and attempted to fit all girls into particular social relationships by force of this assumption.

Burke (1990) explains how "terministic screens" work like different colored photographic lenses to filter attention toward and away from a version of reality:

> Even if any given terminology is a reflection of reality, by its very nature as a terminology it must be a selection of reality; and to this extent it must function also as a deflection of reality. (p. 1035)

The discourse circulating around the focal students constructed such "terministic screens," which seemed to homogenize them and, as will be seen, rendered many of their behaviors invisible to school personnel.

CHAPTER 2

Entering Adolescence: Literacy and Allegiance in Junior High

I turn now to the end of a story: The last weeks in May at a junior high school. I begin here because I believe that an examination of one culminating event reveals the themes and tensions that permeated my year at Northern Hills Junior High School. The distribution of the junior high yearbook serves as a window onto the complex processes that create and constrain, within the school context, social roles that are informed by socioeconomic status, gender, and social-group allegiances. As school years draw to a close, students across the nation anticipate the biggest school-sanctioned literacy event of the year: the sale and distribution of the school yearbook. Like students elsewhere, Northern Hills Junior High students anxiously awaited its arrival.

"A SENSE OF BELONGING": SOCIAL ROLES AND THE YEARBOOK "EVENT"

At Northern Hills, seventh grade marked the year in which students first produced and published a school yearbook, providing, it seems, a signpost of students' entrance into the adolescent arena. Many of these seventh graders bought their first yearbook, a symbol of distinction that separated them from elementary students. As elementary students, they had heard from older siblings and friends about *the junior high yearbook*, and its significance had been made clear since early October, when they were warned by way of intercom announcements to "Order now. Don't wait. Yearbooks will sell out fast."

With yearbook photographers occasionally popping into classrooms and disruptions from the intercom regularly announcing that band members or the volleyball team or the drama club should report to the gym for yearbook photographs, the presence of the yearbook was felt not just in May but throughout the year.

Produced by 65 students working together with the help of two staff advisors, the yearbook, a 48-page soft-bound document, captured the year through photographs, student-produced artwork, and captions. Sports held a prominent place in the pages of the yearbook: Photos of football, track, basketball, and wrestling events for the boys and track, tennis, volleyball, and basketball for the girls filled the pages. The book also contained photos of Soda—a drug and alcohol awareness club—and drama club.

I believe that most teachers would agree with one of the yearbook's faculty advisors, the media specialist, who described the importance of the yearbook this way:

> If you can find your mug in here [yearbook], it gives you a tremendous sense of belonging. We tried to cover all of the major events, and it's important to find yourself. We took a lot of pictures. If you and your mom can find yourself in here, then everything is just A-OK.

Here, the media specialist pointed out the importance of belonging, describing how belonging is documented by a photo in the yearbook. Similarly, Smith (1986) describes the necessity of belonging in regard to literacy learning. Using the metaphor of a "literacy club," he writes:

> And once again, membership in the literacy club adds to the individual's sense of personal identity, of who he or she is. "Hi, kid, you're one of us," say the members of the literacy club. (p. 38)

Borrowing Smith's metaphor, Meyers (1992) examines how students' social relations and thinking processes impinge on each other by categorizing students' uses of literacy within different social contexts as follows: to share membership, to contest membership, to fake membership, and to maintain membership. At Northern Hills, the junior high yearbook served similar functions, documenting membership in what might be considered an adolescent club. I use the term "club" to describe a set of discursive practices that shape and create social roles. As it is used here, a club provides an opportunity to examine the institutional conception of membership, of belonging. Giroux (1992) argues that "student experience will have to be analyzed as part of a wider relationship between culture and power" (p. 16). What implicit cultural attributes encompass becoming "one of us"? What is valued? What roles are made available? How is the organization structured? What privileges and rewards are conferred by such a membership? What are the duties and obligations?

Photographs of after-school club and team activities dominated the book, revealing implicit values: Clearly, high value was placed on extra-curricular participation, team membership, and competition.

Teachers, administrators, and many parents perceived extracurricular involvement as the key to both enjoyment and academic success. The faculty and student handbooks referred to sports, drama, and club activities as "cocurricular" rather than as "extracurricular." While carried on outside the designated school day, these activities were perceived by teachers, administrators, and many parents as central to the school's academic program. When asked what was most beneficial for her daughter during the school year, one mother explained, "After-school sports. I really like them. They keep her involved." This parent, like many others, believed that involvement in after-school activities would have a positive academic impact.

I contend that an examination of the school as a club makes visible disparate positions of status and power. Infused with the discourse of adolescence, the junior high school filters attention toward one particular group of students and, as you will see, renders others invisible.

SOCIAL BOUNDARIES: THE QUEENS AND THE COOKIES

Just a few days before the sale of yearbooks, intercom announcements and rumors of the exact date of arrival revved students up. During second period, Mr. Anson, the building principal, announced, "The yearbooks are not here yet, but we will let you know the moment they get here." "The moment" was enunciated with such clarity that students in Mrs. Zmoleck's language arts class began buzzing with excitement. Mrs. Zmoleck attempted to distract them from the coming attraction. "Okay, it's free-reading time," she announced to counterbalance Mr. Anson on the intercom. For several days, Mr. Anson's morning announcements continued to remind students of the sale of yearbooks— as if any of them could not be keenly aware of the impending arrival.

Teachers' conversations, too, were laced with references to the arrival of the yearbook as they planned for the event. At Northern Hills Junior High, the yearbook had become a central part of the end-of-the-year curriculum. The distribution date seemed to be the only negative concern mentioned by teachers, who feared that an early release date might sabotage their scheduled plans for "signing time" in class during the last week of school. They talked to each other about the need to save the yearbook for the last week so it would fit within their curricular calendar. For the most part, teachers described the yearbook as a celebration and a well-earned reward for a year of hard work. They allocated class time for signing and sharing yearbooks. Perceived as a way to control the behavior of the 531 seventh and eighth graders who in late May might not be eager to participate in discussions or complete end-of-semester projects, signing time was a tool for negotiating with students, often appearing as a bribe. Teachers told students: "If we get all our work done . . . ," "If you are all good . . . ," "If you cooperate, and we can hurry through this . . . " The following teacher comment received several nods and "me toos" from staff in the teacher's lounge: "I give them the last five to ten minutes to write depending on how the class goes. It's a reward. It's a privilege. It's their reward for good behavior."

When the book was sold one full week before the last day of the school year, several teachers expressed frustration: "What are we going to do with them the last week? Students won't have anything to do"; "It gives them something to do at the end of school." Teachers explained that all the students looked forward to receiving the book, and that this sense of urgency might have forced the early sales.

The yearbook played such a large part in the end-of-school activities because the teachers and administrators all believed, as the media specialist articulated, that it gave a tremendous sense of belonging. The discourse of adolescence that privileges peer-group allegiances constructed filters, it seems, that prevented school personnel from seeing the yearbook as exclusionary. Although the yearbook was viewed as a symbol of solidarity for all students, only a particular population of students was made to feel as if they belonged to this club. Other students remained outsiders.

Having provided insight into the role of the yearbook from the institutional perspective, I turn now to the focal students themselves, describing the day of arrival of the yearbook from their perspective.

The Arrival of the Yearbook: Tiffany's Scene

It was lunch time, but students crowded the hallway outside the cafeteria. Crouched down in bunches, girls giggled, shrieked, and tipped one another over as they huddled together to sign each other's books. Boys and girls leaned against lockers or used a friend's back to steady a book for signing. Yearbooks flew across the corridor with a verbal "Hey, sign mine," tagged onto them.

It was easy to hear Tiffany's voice above the loud chatter. She leaped up from a crowd of girls, her long red hair flying back as she cackled loudly and ran full speed to the end of the hall, sloshing small amounts of her chocolate malt across the tan carpet as she went. She slammed into a group of friends and yanked a yearbook from one boy's hand, screaming, "Whose's this? You want me to sign it, don't you?" She looked over her shoulder at me, shouting, "I just have to keep writing until they'll let me stop. Everybody wants me to sign their book." She grinned and plopped herself down in the middle of the group. Like a pile of puppies, her friends pushed up against each other as she elbowed them over and wriggled her way in.

The Arrival of the Yearbook: Cleo's Scene

Inside, the cafeteria was much less crowded on that day. The large room was nearly empty and particularly quiet. I scanned the room and found Cleo and her friends in their usual seats in the middle of the front section, "the woof-woof tables," as Tiffany's friends described the area. Without difficulty, because there were so few students in the area, I made my way to them and stuffed my backpack under the table. Beth, Pat, Cleo, and Dottie were eating in silence. Not one yearbook was visible at their table. Sensing the awkwardness of the silence, I did not ask about it. Instead, I mentioned the rainy weather, and Dottie complained that she and her mother had worked late the night before, trimming all the tall, wet grass from around their trailer so they wouldn't be charged a penalty fee by the trailer-park management. Lunch continued with talk about rain, cookies, and favorite flavors of malts.

After lunch, I asked Cleo privately about the yearbooks. "Oh, I'm not very interested in them," she reported. When I reminded her that she had told me a week before that she thought she'd get one, she just shrugged her shoulders and repeated that she wasn't interested: "I don't know why I would want one. None of my friends are in there anyway."

The literacy event surrounding the arrival of the yearbook appears very different when one looks through the eyes of Tiffany and Cleo. These two scenes illustrate sharp contrasts between the two groups of girlfriends.

The yearbook was one mechanism that created tangible boundaries between groups. Students used photos and messages to assess status and document allegiances. One powerful position within the school was that of yearbook staff member. Many considered it an honor to be a member of the yearbook staff and especially to be one of the eighth-grade photographers, who were allowed to leave study halls throughout the year to snap candid shots of the student body. This position held power because it carried the privilege of added mobility around the school and access to other classrooms. Most important, individuals who held this position acted as gatekeepers, controlling who populated the pages of the yearbook.

The queens literally counted the number of photos each had in the yearbook, using the number as a measurement of popularity. When the yearbook arrived, these girls quickly flipped through the pages looking for themselves and their friends as proof of their belonging. On the other hand, Cleo's remark, "None of my friends are in there anyway," makes it clear that the cookies were aware of their absence.

Tiffany's and Cleo's networks of friends seemed to have very little in common. Tiffany loved to socialize. Her friends were active in athletic events, attended school activities and dances, and spent much of their leisure time together with same-age peers. In contrast, Cleo, like her friends, spent most of her leisure time with her family. She did not participate in any extracurricular activities and preferred to spend her time at home.

Constant comments from Northern Hills staff that "Everybody gets one" and "Everyone loves them" reveal that Cleo and Dottie and many others were invisible to school personnel. Current enrollment was 531; 425 books were ordered. Eight were sold to adults, 10 were distributed as complimentary copies, 10 were mailed to students who no longer lived in the district, and 5 remained unsold. In all, 397 copies were sold to students, which left 134 students without yearbooks. That figure represents 25% of the total student population. While students may not have purchased a yearbook for a variety of reasons, the socioeconomic status of families may have been a critical issue. For whatever reason, when teachers rewarded students with "signing time," one out of four students was not able to participate.

Economic constraints prevented some students from fully participating in the culture of the school and from participating in the biggest school-sanctioned literacy event of the year. This lack of a sense of belonging, of shared culture, was a constant tension in the conversations of Cleo, her family, and her friends. Cleo and Dottie lived in trailer parks, which in the Midwest carries a stigma that spills over into the school context, where some teachers and some administrators perceive that such living arrangements lead to school problems.

At times, it was not simply a matter of economics that interfered with the institution's construction of full participation in school activities, but the perceptions of economic status that others brought to the school context. This attitude was more fully illustrated by the principal's comments about students who come from trailer parks, which he described as "places that are too closely knit. They live too closely together. They know each other's problems and that causes problems at school." Likewise, constructions of the social dimension of schooling created obstacles for some students. At Northern Hills, I often heard the category "trailer-park kids" used to connote a lack of appropriate social skills in particular students. Some teachers described their class makeup in terms of numbers of students from trailer parks. A teacher's comment such as "I've got seven trailer-park kids" conveyed to other teachers the implicit yet clearly understood assumption of impending trouble for that teacher.

While economic resources played a major part in determining who would participate more fully in ways that the school had constructed participation, there was much evidence to suggest that an equal if not greater factor was the circulation of what Bourdieu (1977) calls cultural capital: the attitudes, beliefs, cultural background, knowledge, and skills that are passed from one generation to the next. In order to understand the cultural capital that each girl carried to school, I turn now to their homes.

Perspectives from the Homes of the Social Queens

Tiffany and Angie were prominent members of this school's "club," clearly evidenced by the fact that each had four pictures in the yearbook. Besides her "mug shot," Tiffany appeared in team pictures with the volleyball team and the basketball team. She also appeared on the collage pages with her arms thrown around Lauren at the fall school dance. All of her best friends appeared throughout the book in candid shots and in volleyball, basketball, and track pictures.

While Tiffany's parents were concerned when her social life interfered with academics, they both explained that it was the cocurricular activities, especially sports, that were helping to shape her in a positive way. They attributed Tiffany's success in school to a great extent to her participation in extracurricular activities, and they encouraged her to undertake every opportunity that was available to her. "She's a very social person. With sports and friends and all," her mother told me. Later in the year, her father attributed her school-year success to this fact:

> I think overall it's been successful because of participating in extra-curricular activities. That's been good for her, not only physically

but mentally. But I personally didn't think I'd survive this year with her, from the standpoint of the constantly, about every other week, getting a letter from the school about this or that, incomplete assignments or whatever just due to her social butterfly attitude she had throughout the year, you know.

Notice the values placed on the benefits of extracurricular activities, "not only physically but mentally." While her father acknowledged that her "social butterfly attitude" caused some difficulties at home due to the demands it entailed (making driving arrangements, attending sporting events and social functions, and occasionally dealing with incomplete assignments), he accepted them as healthy signs of this developmental period. The discourse of adolescence reverberates in Tiffany's father's words. Letters from school, incomplete assignments, along with the social butterfly attitude, signaled to him that Tiffany was a normal adolescent.

Like Tiffany, Angie was actively involved in the school's social life. She participated in volleyball, basketball, and track as well as chorus and weight-lifting. Angie's mother described her, too, as social:

A big part of her life's her social life. She's involved in a lot of things. It's an important part of school, in terms of learning because if you've got a happy child, all around happy child, she's going to do better at everything. Probably doesn't need to be quite as involved as she is, but she needs it. I think it's important to have extracurricular activities to keep her happy.

Parents of the queens expressed concern that there simply wasn't as much time for reading or family now that they were in junior high, but they strongly supported the importance of extracurricular activities as a direct route to school success: physically, socially, and academically.

Perspectives from the Homes of the Tough Cookies

Missing from the yearbook were any pictures other than the official "mug shots" of Cleo, Dottie, or their friends. Tough cookies did not participate in any extracurricular activities and were invisible to the eighth-grade photographers who were busy throughout the year taking candid shots around school.

Even purchasing a yearbook created tension. Consider Cleo's mother's frustration with her inability to send $8.00 to school so her daughter could have a yearbook to sign like all the other girls. Torn between the pressures of stretching a tight budget and wanting her daughter to belong, she said:

> I do not understand. I do not understand why they assume that everybody has tons of money, and every time I turn around it's more money for this and more money for that. Where do they get the idea that we've got all this money?

Like Cleo, Dottie had a picture only in the mug-shot section. Like Cleo's mother, Dottie's mother did not have the economic resources to allow Dottie to participate fully in school in ways the school might have envisioned. For instance, after Dottie's language arts teacher encouraged her to try out for the fall play, her mother explained to me why she did not "choose" to participate: "I think Dottie told you that we don't have a car right now. She's embarrassed and doesn't want her teachers to know."

Understanding the social dimensions of this condition go far beyond any economic factors. While Cleo's mother may have regretted that Cleo did not get a yearbook and Dottie's mother might have liked Dottie to try out for the play, both women regularly expressed values that conflicted with the sense of belonging that permeated the messages surrounding the sale of the yearbook. Cleo's mother explained her anxiety and worries in the move to junior high:

> The biggest thing for me is the social stuff. I'm not ready for her to move outside the family, and it's hard for me to say, "yeah, you can do it," because I don't feel comfortable yet.

Later in the same interview, she told me that she planned for her daughter to attend a nearby college so she can remain at home. She explained the importance of family in this way:

> Like the Orientals and even the Indian people, [I think] families are most important. And everybody works together to get wherever they're going. And I really don't think that us, as White people or whatever, I don't think we do that. I think we just start cutting off, saying you're on your own, you know. And I really do think that families should always stick together as long as possible. I mean you give them a boost up. I don't like that boot-out stuff.

In opposition to the discourse of adolescence, which privileges allegiance with same-age peers, this quote reveals a continued emphasis on close ties with significant adults. Unlike parents of the social queens, who regarded severing ties with adults as a sign of normal progression into adolescence, the parents of the cookies regarded maintaining allegiances with family as central. Emphasis on maintaining family ties in working-class families during adolescence is documented elsewhere (Schlegel & Barry, 1991; Weiss, 1993). McRobbie's (1978) study documents the centrality of home and family life for working-class girls. I argue that one must account for marked differential role constructions that accompany the move into adolescence. In the school setting, it seems that adolescence as a life stage may have constructed filters that deny diversity.

Cleo's mother regularly made sharp contrasts between academic and social aspects of schooling. She explained, "I want Cleo to be educated. I don't want her to be social." Like Cleo's mother, Dottie's mother discouraged her daughter from participating in any cocurricular activities: "Maybe when she is in high school, 16 or 17, then she can do track or something. *Not now!*"

Both women expressed a strong distrust of the social side of schooling and presented a set of values that conflicted with Northern Hills teachers' thinking about appropriate pedagogy for the language arts classroom. (Note the importance of peer response and collaborative groups in reading and writing workshops in the work of Atwell, 1987, and Graves, 1983.) Both women deemphasized the importance of peer groups. Both mothers strongly resisted the notion that social activities were a part of the educational process or a sign of progression into the developmental stage of adolescence.

"SIGN MINE": CONSTRUCTING IDENTITY AND CLAIMING ALLEGIANCE

Time to write in the school yearbook was perceived as a reward by teachers, and students often announced that this sanctioned writing time was their right, demanding time to scrawl their messages across the face of another student.

Literacies—both sanctioned literacies and literate underlife—served to maintain particular social roles and document particular allegiances. At Northern Hills, writing in the yearbook provides a unique opportunity to examine the dimensions of sanctioned literacies (those that are recognized and circulated by adults in authority) and literate underlife (those literate practices that are out of sight and out of control of those in authority, practices in opposition to the institution). Within the pages of the yearbook, literate practices marked membership and measured status within social groups. Messages were borrowed, erased, and scribbled over to present a particular kind of self as well as to document and deny allegiances. Six pages were included at the back for just such writing practices. Clearly, writing in the yearbook privileged those who matched the dominant image of the adolescent, both economically and culturally. The cookies are absent from the remaining discussion.

Presenting a particular self through their literate choices, boys' inscriptions centered on action while girls' messages focused on relationships. Messages such as "Your [sic] a total babe," "Yo, The spirit 40 lives on," and "Stay sweet and sexy, NOT" found their way onto these pages. Just as the sixth-grade girls in Cherland's (1994) study used dress, demeanor, and leisure-time activities (including reading) as a way to "do gender," signing the yearbook was a means of marking gender. Drawing on West and Zimmerman (1987), Cherland writes that "doing gender involves a complex of socially guided perceptual, interactional, and micropolitical activities that cast particular pursuits as expressions of masculine and feminine 'natures'" (p. 12). Of the messages printed above, "Your [sic] a total babe" and "Yo, The spirit 40 lives on" were written by males, while "Stay sweet and sexy, NOT" was written by seventh-grade girls. The boys often inscribed their basketball jersey number into their messages: "The spirit 40 lives on." Although many girls participated in basketball, no reference to sports was evident in their yearbook inscriptions.

Both boys and girls sought to affix a kind of permanence to their messages. Yearbook inscriptions served, it seems, to secure one's role and relationships in print. "Forever" and "lives on" appeared in an overwhelming majority of messages. Girls most often signed their inscriptions with B.F.F. (Best Friends Forever) while boys secured their social position by such comments as "Yo, #15 Forever" and "We're #1 forever." In these attempts to attach permanence to a presentation of self, such signatures were clearly declarations of cultural masculine and feminine identification: Boys sought to present a competitive self while girls sought attachment with others.

Romance marked the signatures of the seventh-grade girls. They often searched for red and pink pens with which to write and dotted their I's with hearts. The girls often drew hearts around boys' pictures and wrote "Love," carefully turning the letter O into a small red heart near a particular boy's picture.

Boys' inscriptions focused on action and on power, presenting the male self as a powerful competitor at the top of the social hierarchy.

Girls, in contrast, presented the self through the male gaze, finding a place in the social order through one's ability to attract male attention: "Stay sweet and sexy" was the most common inscription for girls.

Some yearbooks were considered to be "ruined" by boys who wrote comments that girls feared would result in punishment at home. Comments such as "Hey, Boobs, I hope I see ALOT of you this summer" created bursts of muffled anger in groups of girls, yet the girls refused to tell adults about such practices and quickly hushed each other up so a teacher would not approach them. Similar to the Oak Town girls in Cherland's 1994 study, the Northern Hills girls never reported such acts. Cherland writes of similar acts of sexual harassment:

> Instead of telling the child what she must do, the culture tells her what she is (Bourdieu, 1991). MTV, the television news, novels, fashion advertisements, older relatives and the boys at school all told Oak Town girls what they were: powerless people whose bodies were "naturally" the object of others' desires. It is not surprising, therefore, that most accepted the practice of sexual harassment. Bourdieu suggests that people come to accept these violent suggestions inscribed in the practices of everyday life, no matter what their status or class, and no matter what the effect on them, because cultural discourses position them as people who must accept the warning, while they in turn come to interpret themselves as those who must submit. In this way, domination is sustained through interpersonal relations, and symbolic violence is accepted as legitimate. (p. 42)

While Northern Hills girls expressed outrage about certain boys' writing practices, they continued to ask Stevie, "the one who ruined that yearbook," to "sign mine" and granted status to the girl who was the victim of the message. Clearly, this comment can be read as a way boys exert control over girls. But trained by the larger culture, the Northern Hills girls received it as a mark of distinction, accepting their position as powerless people defined through their body images.

Gossip about the comment carried much currency for several days. While the Northern Hills male presented the self as a powerful actor, he represented the female as object of desire. The early adolescent girl accepts his representation of her as an object, more specifically as an anatomical commodity.

Although this particular comment was made invisible, by blocking it out with a thick black marker, the seventh graders continued to regard its presence. Under the black ink was the secret sexual message that was revealed to those deemed an appropriate audience. Girls led each other by the hand to the yearbook, "See, this is where it is." The phrase was repeated in present tense: "where it is," not "where it was." The sexual message remained present under the black marker. As children, these girls accepted sexuality as taboo; yet, as early adolescents, they sought to enact a sexual self through their literate practices. Although hidden from adults, the message was not erased. It was not erased from the yearbook or from the construction of identity that these girls were internalizing.

PATROLLING THE BORDERS: LITERACY AS RITUAL OF EXCLUSION

KATIE: Can I sign your yearbook?
BARB: No.

A quick glance at the yearbook shows row after row of white faces ordered by alphabetical arrangement. The seeming homogeneity conceals diversity: Invisible barriers such as attitudes, beliefs, economics, and experiences separate these young people into at least two camps. The girls created markers to maintain the borders between them. Allegiances became visible in both the act of writing and in the messages themselves. What is written and to whom is controlled by one's social status. Yearbooks circulated across social boundaries, yet those with the greatest social status stood in judgment of those less powerful. Students carefully monitored who could sign their yearbooks. To allow one of lesser status to mark one's book appeared to lower the status of the book owner. Students often asked for and were denied signing privileges. The cookies did not participate in signing, and within the queens' friendship network, a hierarchy was clearly visible. Some students were in fact told "No," after asking, "Can I sign your yearbook?" In the same way, some students refused to sign yearbooks of those perceived to be outside the circle of significance. Who had the right to write was clearly an issue of entitlement defined by Shuman (1986) as "the rights of both addressors and addressees, as well as to the onlookers, witnesses, eavesdroppers and third-party listeners to a message, as well as the characters in the message" (p. 18). If one was perceived as an outsider, then one was not entitled to write. Likewise, one might or might not be entitled to even view the message. Students guarded their written texts and controlled who had the right to see them.

The issue of entitlement, according to Shuman (1993), concerns one's rights to "appropriate another's voice as a means of borrowing authority, whether in an act of complicity or resistance to that authority" (p. 136). Messages inscribed in the yearbook illustrate positions of both compliance and resistance—most often compliance to peers deemed higher in social status and resistance to adults. Layers of authority become visible when one examines these written texts. For example, as an act of resistance, one student parodied Mr. Tibidioux, her language arts teacher, taking that teacher's own words to mock his authority: "It is clear that . . ." Borrowing these words from his recurring instruction for writing appropriate responses, she wrote them in a yearbook and then, to claim publicly that she knew that he was leaving the school system at the close of the year, she added, "It is clear that Scooby-doo [rhymes with Tibidioux] is leaving," spoofing his name and his practice. Standing in judgment, the queens erased some teachers' pictures altogether. To exercise their authority over others, they drew over and scribbled on teachers' images and those of other students.

Students with the greatest status were freed from judgment, and their written comments became models for others to copy. As I watched, one student carefully moved her finger across the page, working cautiously to transfer a phrase exactly from one yearbook to another. Because a particular phrase was perceived as carrying more currency in this arena, this teen appropriated the words of another student as her own in order for her own voice to contain that power. Students shared texts and at times took another person's message for their own, copying the same phrase from one yearbook to the next to the next. In such borrowing of texts, one, in a sense, borrowed the social status of another. In taking another's message as her own, each girl had to be careful not to overstep her boundaries, and, as Shuman (1986) suggests, write what she was not entitled to write.

In the act of writing, students inadvertently may mark themselves as outsiders by writing a message judged inappropriate by others. If one was not savvy enough to create an appropriate text or powerful enough to forgo judgment, often, out of fear of marking oneself as outsider, one just scribbled safe messages such as "Have a good summer" or "See ya next year."

Some students, in order to preserve their social position, asked a friend, "What should I write? What do you want me to say?" Students took this opportunity to exert their position of authority and made such playful comments as "Say I'm 'just too cool'" or "Say 'she's always got a taco'" (a current description for shorts or jeans that were considered too tight across the seat of the pants) or "Write, 'BFF ASS'" (a code for best friends forever and always stay sweet or sexy). Many comments were so highly coded that only those few insiders could translate them.

In order for students to demonstrate that they were with it, comments carrying the current pop jargon taken from movies, television, or local sources become etched into this school-sanctioned document, creating an unusual juxtaposition of sanctioned and out-of-bounds literacies. Dark, graffiti-like messages boldly cut across the white-bordered layout and quite literally "defaced" students and teachers alike. With big pink erasers, students rubbed out the faces of outsiders.

Constructing a dual set of standards as a way to separate themselves from adults and from children, the queens at times judged their yearbook writing as appropriate for their friends but too obscene to share with parents, teachers, or those outside their social network. Adhering to the adolescent code, the queens sought to present a sexual self, lacing romance and sexual innuendo into their messages. They reported to me that such topics were appropriate for them as teenagers and continued to hide them from parents and teachers.

In all of this writing, the queens demonstrated a tremendous sense of play. Signing yearbooks had the feeling of recess, providing playtime away from the institutional demands of schooling, away from adult supervision. Similar to the playground, who could play was controlled by the peer dynamic. The yearbook was used to stake out territory and control social interactions. Yearbook messages regulated relationships and interests. In these ways, yearbook writing served two purposes: to construct a border around particular adolescents and to measure growth into adulthood.

EMBRACING ADOLESCENCE: THE YEARBOOK AS PROCESS AND OBJECT

The yearbook provided a pictorial history, freezing moments of friendship, of athletic prowess, of academic endeavors. It provided, too, a unique opportunity to blur the boundaries between school-sanctioned literacies and literate underlife: sanctioned time in the school context given over to leisure, words written publicly yet secretly and quite literally written across the faces of authority while under the watchful gaze of those in authority. For seventh graders here, it was their first yearbook, a symbol of membership in the junior high school and entry into an adolescent arena: photos published as proof of sanctioned membership in the junior high, words scribbled across those pages as proof of the unsanctioned resistance that marks one as adolescent.

As a member of any club, one accepts the rules and obligations of the organization in order to enjoy the rights and benefits that accompany such a membership. Membership in the junior high "club" carried dues; competition and cocurricular participation were a central part of such obligations. In other words, one must embrace or at least comply with the roles that such a membership enlists.

Belonging to the Northern Hills district is a privilege that few parents or teachers would refute. With top standardized test scores and a near zero dropout rate, Northern Hills is looked on as a highly successful, fully functioning district. A full array of cocurricular opportunities, well-kept grounds and facilities, abundant instructional materials, and low student-teacher ratios serve as markers of school success that carry across state lines and distinguish the Northern Hills Community School District as one of the finest in the nation. Northern Hills, fully entitled to call itself a place of pride, closely matches an idealized school. Yet, do we fully understand the implications of this match? Terry Eagleton (1991) writes:

> In the field of education, for example, symbolic violence operates not so much by the teacher speaking "ideologically" to the students, but by the teacher being perceived as in possession of an amount of "cultural capital" which the student needs to acquire. The educational system thus contributes to reproducing the dominant social order not so much by the viewpoint it fosters, but by this regulated distribution of cultural capital . . . those who lack the "correct" taste are unobtrusively excluded, relegated to shame and silence. (pp. 157–58)

I contend that it is not the teacher alone but the entire institution and larger community that distribute a pervasive cultural capital. As a "Place of Pride," Northern Hills articulates a progressivism that characterizes its curriculum; yet such an insistent argument masks the traditional remnants that persist under the surface. When we examine school as a symbol of membership in a larger culture, we uncover a powerful ideology that continues to privilege the dominant class and insists on maintaining the status quo. The junior high comes equipped with one way of being in the world. The junior high school arena requires the strong sense of competition and team membership that permeated the pages of the yearbook. To resist the demands of this adolescent organization marks one as less than a fully functioning member.

I would argue that the characteristics of adolescence as a developmental stage are not so much a part of this stage because they are biologically wired or psychologically triggered. They emerge because they are ideological constructs that are fostered by the schedule and structure of the junior high school. Beyond economics, the emphasis at Northern Hills on cocurricular activities that fill up after-school, evening, and weekend hours requires children to realign their positions within their family structure. A focus on winning both in the classroom and on the athletic field nurtured a keen focus on the self. Thus, to fully participate in this club, earning the privileges that it entails, demanded strong same-age social networks, severing or at least distancing from parental ties, and placing emphasis on a competitive self, all highly prized by Northern Hills standards. Members in good standing met such demands. Anyone who was unwilling or unable to meet them was marginalized.

The junior high yearbook packed the ideology of the school district and the larger culture into its 48 pages, translating a set of values into images and texts that were carried through the halls and through the community. Looking back at the yearbook as literacy event, looking through the eyes of Cleo and Tiffany, the yearbook takes on significance both as process (ideological inculcation) and object (cultural capital).

Throughout this examination of the yearbook as event, it becomes clear that while the discourse of adolescence denies diversity, those complexities, however subtle, do exist, creating invisible obstacles. A vast tangle of competing expectations and allegiances shapes the school context, which in turn shapes social roles. As an actual event and as a larger symbol, the school yearbook illustrates how one's membership constricts and enables particular literate practices that in turn constrict and enable particular roles available to group members.

Conceived of as an opportunity for all to celebrate the completion of another successful academic year, the yearbook provided much more. It served as a marker. For Tiffany and the other social queens it reaffirmed their position in the school arena and in the larger community. They measured their status by the number and size of their pictures and by the number of requests to sign books: "Everybody wants me to sign their book." For Cleo and her friends, it also reaffirmed their position: "None of my friends are in there anyway."

The role of the yearbook within the institutional context remains central to the closing of the school year. The yearbook stands as an icon. Unknowingly, some are allowed to speak while others are silenced, some to write while others are written upon.

CHAPTER 3

Literacy and the Social Queens

The social fabric of the social queens was woven together with literate threads. The group used literacy to lace its members tightly together and exclude those beyond their circle of significance. The nature of this group's social interactions created rigid standards used to measure and moderate appropriate behaviors both within and outside of the school context. Their rules and rituals were most often mediated through written texts and were used to govern specific roles available within the school context. The unifying thread of their relationships was an unfaltering allegiance to a group identity.

At home and at school, social-group identity was privileged. Concealing individual differences, the queens created social roles through a group lens. Debra Zmoleck, a seventh-grade language arts teacher, explained: "Most seventh-grade girls, even if they are A students, are not independent . . . I mean it's like, 'Yes, I want my A, but I'm going to try to figure out how to get that around being social, around doing all the fun things.'"

THE LIFEWORLD OF THE SOCIAL QUEENS

"Doing all the fun things" and "being social" characterized the ways in which the queens constructed their roles at home and at school. Ways of being social were for the most part enacted as ways of appearing and being the same. The girls quickly hid distinguishing marks. Because group identity was privileged over individual identity, allegiance to peer group remained central. The queens seemed to perform as members of what Goffman (1959) called "performance teams," defined as "any set of individuals who co-operate in staging a single routine" (p. 79). Physical appearance, dress, social behavior, academic achievement, and reading and writing preferences were carefully monitored by the girls to present a unified front. Not only did these girls arrange their hair and

48

dress similarly, but on weekends they exchanged grocery bags full of clothing so that the next week each girl could come to school dressed in the same outfits as those of her tight circle of friends.

The queens' primary reason for being at school could be located in the social realm. For these adolescents, school was most often perceived as a social arena, a time to connect with friends and make arrangements for after-school activities. Sports, dances, and clubs blurred the borders of the school day. Such school functions allowed for a smooth flow between the school and home contexts. For these girls, the social aspects of junior high life far outweighed the academic. Attendance at school was regarded as important primarily for social-group participation. Academics were, for the most part, perceived as opportunities to document allegiances within peer networks.

Tiffany and Angie regularly boasted that teachers couldn't tell them apart if they were not together. In an interview, Angie remarked, "Ms. Jacobsen said that she didn't know me anymore cause I wasn't with Tiff." This was a source of pride among the friends, who resisted marking any distinctions among themselves. They hedged their opinions unless they were sure of at least partial consensus from members within their friendship circle. In language arts class, for example, when students were asked to list their favorite book on an interest inventory, Tiffany leaned over to ask a friend, "What's my favorite book?" On another occasion, Carrie asked Angie whether she should raise her hand. After receiving a reinforcing nod from Angie, she then raised her hand to tell Mr. Tibidioux, "It's hard for us to hear back here."

Teachers, too, grouped these friends together and, in fact, commented that "It's hard to tell them apart when they are not in their seats." Such comments enhanced a sense of group identity that these girls worked very hard to cultivate. Most of the time teachers referred to each girl as "one of the popular crowd" or jokingly called them "the fashion police."

Teachers at times compared academic achievements within the group. "Angie works harder than Tiffany," Mr. Tibidioux, their seventh-grade language arts teacher, said on many occasions. "Angie is a better student than Tiffany." Regularly citing the power of peer influence among members of this friendship network, teachers attributed academic success to peers. For example, when Angie's grade showed a marked decline and her interest in class activities appeared to decrease, Mr. Tibidioux remarked, "She is really being influenced by Tiffany right now. She's struggling to decide between Tiffany and school. I hope Tiffany doesn't bring her way down. I hope that she is strong enough." Her language arts teacher saw her achievement level as a direct result of her close association with Tiffany, whom he saw as a less-motivated student, and so he attributed Angie's slipping directly to her friend. Of course, the queens' insistence of a unified front directly supported Mr. Tibidioux's perceptions.

At the junior high setting, there was little opportunity for teachers to learn that in Angie's household, discussions of divorce and the possibility of moving in with a grandmother could have been an equal if not greater factor in Angie's loss of motivation for schoolwork. Constrained by limited contact time with students, teachers had few opportunities to learn of students' life experiences that might affect behaviors within the classroom. The fact that students were rarely well known by their teachers added to the dynamics of this group's performance: Each social queen was perceived of as a member of the group rather than as an individual girl with a complex life history.

As I attempted to avoid presenting a singular image of these friends, I, too, struggled to find distinctions among members in a group that denied difference. Guided by images of beauty and sexuality transported through print and other media, the queens attempted to fit themselves into a singular standard of feminine adolescence as a measure of their own growth into adulthood. Such assumptions of sameness were fostered by the discourse of adolescence, which promotes a singular adolescent model, a model embraced by the social queens.

The social queens valued their friendship group over almost everything else. They spent as much leisure time together as their mothers would allow and regarded being alone as a punishment. Their weekends were filled with social engagements such as attending movies, sleeping over, and shopping. With basketball and volleyball practice and games on weeknights, there was little time away from friends. During the five-minute passing time between classes at school, queens rushed together, gathering at a locker to apply hair spray to their bangs and exchange the notes written during the previous class. As the following comment reveals, both Angie and Lauren believed that they were most comfortable when they were with friends:

M.F.: Angie, in what situations do you feel most comfortable and most yourself?
ANGIE: When I'm with Tiffany and Lauren.

The girls all but refused to be interviewed alone. As a group, they appeared confident, outgoing, boisterous, at the edge of haughty. Alone, each girl appeared quieter, much less confident, and generally answered any number of questions with "I don't know." The contrast between an individual voice alone in a room and an individual voice in the presence of peers was striking, as the following transcript reveals. In a final exit interview, I presented Tiffany with a list of the books that she had checked out from the junior high library for the entire academic year. Her voice at first was so quiet it was difficult to transcribe.

M.F.: So, what's the difference between Christopher Pike and R. L. Stine?

TIFFANY: I don't know. Christopher Pike books are like, I don't know they are like longer. I don't know maybe more detail. I don't know, I guess, I like, I don't know. These are just like. I don't know. These [R. L. Stine novels] are just quick.

M.F. [pointing to the library list]: Is any one of these better than the rest?

TIFFANY: I don't know.

M.F.: Which one did you like best?

TIFFANY: I don't know. Oh, I don't remember one, two, and three [reference to books in the R. L. Stine series]. I don't know. I never read *Honey I Blew Up the Kids*. [Lauren barges into the study room. Tiffany's voice becomes louder and more animated. To Lauren] You are annoying!

LAUREN: Oh, thanks.

TIFFANY: I mean good annoying, not like Carrie. Now, she is annoying all the time. Have you seen Carrie's legs like she went wild with the razor? She's all cut up. She's got scratches all over.

Notice the opening ritual between Lauren and Tiffany. Tiffany's greeting was regarded by both as a playful attack on Lauren's character. The girls then connected by drawing attention to the flaws in one of their closest friends, Carrie. The conversation continued as follows:

LAUREN [to me]: She didn't read that [points to the book on top of Tiffany's notebook, *Gimme Kisses*, a novel written by Christopher Pike].

TIFFANY: That's a good book! *Gimme Kisses*!

LAUREN: *Gimme Kisses*? That's a good book?

M.F.: A little bit ago I think you said that Christopher Pike isn't quite as good as Stine?

TIFFANY: Well I got Christopher Pike. That's Christopher Pike right there, *Gimme Kisses*, and I like it and everything.

LAUREN: R. L. Stine is like a lot more interesting.

TIFFANY: Christopher Pike is like really confusing. A lot of his books
    are.
LAUREN: Like *Bury Me Deep*, that is kind of confusing.
TIFFANY: Yeah, you have to go really like slow.
LAUREN: I know cause it took Tiffany about a week to read that.
TIFFANY: Yeah, like Angie warned me. She goes, "That's a confusing
    book, go slow." It is like all right. I had to ask Angie questions
    about what is going on.

In the above transcript it is evident that Lauren's arrival gave Tiffany
a voice. In Tiffany's first answer, she hedged with six "I don't knows."
With Lauren present, Tiffany spoke louder and was more willing to
state her opinion because she was not alone in it. Her opinion was
greatly shaped by Lauren's presence.

Throughout the year, when any two social queens came together, I
observed this ritual of attacking the character or appearance of one who
was not present. Likewise, when anyone left the area, talk generally
focused on a critique of that particular girl's physical appearance or
recent behavior. I asked them about my recurring observations of this
ritual near the end of the school year. Lauren was not present during
this interview.

M.F.: What is it with you that every time someone leaves, everybody
    thinks they are talking about them?
TIFFANY: Because they are.
ANGIE: Because they are.
TIFFANY: Whenever Lauren leaves everybody goes, "God, I hate it
    when she does this and this."
ANGIE: Remember when we all spent the night at Carrie's. We spent
    the whole night talking about Lauren.
TIFFANY: We talked about her like mad.
ANGIE: The *WHOLE* night.

Such gossip allows one to both relate and evaluate experiences (Britton, 1970, p. 110). Gossip (and I use the term to connote private talk
about the experiences of others) was such a prevalent and overt practice
that the queens traveled in packs to avoid being the target of such
discussion. On numerous occasions, they told me directly that missing
a party or dance or sleepover meant they would be the subject of such
talk. During adolescence, when rules of behavior are unclear, this gossip is used to establish and clarify norms, norms that for the queens

were extremely rigid. Such gossip, which to adults may seem quite negative, was used to check and test adolescent rules. Some researchers refer to early adolescence as a period of paranoia in which the focus of attention is so much on the self that there is a tendency for these early teens to falsely assume that all eyes are on them (Santrock, 1993). Of course, in light of this ritualized practice, it is hardly surprising that each girl might assume a conversation was about her.

While the queens always insisted that there were not any "rules" to follow, that each simply had individually chosen to do, to wear, to read, to write what she did, there was remarkable evidence to the contrary. While each girl worked to identify herself as a nonindividualized member of her friendship network, social hierarchies emerged. When I pushed them to mark themselves as individuals, they noted assets or limitations of each other that cast one another into a higher or lower social status. In some research on gender there appears to be a tendency to normalize and idealize a presumably female way with words (Belenky et al., 1986; Gilligan, 1988). Such work on gender articulates that women and girls use language to connect rather than to compete and that patterns of talk are relational rather than hierarchical. In contrast, Mrs. Zmoleck acknowledged the gender differences that she observed in her 17 years of teaching seventh and eighth graders at Northern Hills in this way:

Seems likes boys are cruel to each other, but when they do it, it's always with fun, laughter, you know, all of this is a big joke. And not that that makes it less cruel, but that's the way they tend to be. You know, it's a big joke, but it's out there. And girls tend to cover theirs up. I mean they are pretty blunt and direct and its like, "There is no joke here. I am just plain mean to you." Whereas a lot of times the boys do it, they cloak it in humor. And I don't think it is any less cruel, but girls just go for the kill.

Confirming evidence from field notes and transcripts support two recurring themes that are reflected in Mrs. Zmoleck's analysis of the girls' behavior: first, as she stated, "the girls tend to cover theirs up," and second, although the queens deny such practices in public, these girls all did cast difference with a competitive edge. In public, the queens presented a unified front. Behind closed doors, in private conversations, allegiances were at times called into question. Backstage, the queens disagreed, competed, blamed and denied allegiance as a way to check and test ways of being adolescent. Such information was publicly concealed and generally transmitted through a private channeling system from one friend to the next to the next. Lauren, for example, wrote in a note, "Yeah, Angie is pretty. She has a perfect face but her hips are too wide."

Goffman (1959) describes backstage regions as places where "the performer can relax; he can drop his front, forgo speaking his lines, and step out of character" (p. 112). Yet, never completely able to, as Goffman suggests, "step out of character" backstage, the queens performed for each other. Such performances most often centered upon body images and attractiveness to boys. These girls used competition to connect. Less apparent in public, competition was allocated to backstage regions. When one girl physically left, the remaining girls made derogatory comments about her to form close bonds with the remaining girls in the room. When these friends came together, they made competitive comments about someone who was not present to draw those present together. This practice was clearly understood and regularly acknowledged by those who practiced it. Competition was central to their relationships.

LITERATE PRACTICES

When one examines the literate practices of the social queens, the same keen sense of competition emerges. Issues of power and status along with group solidarity became visible. Because of the nature of this group's social network, literacy was of central importance, serving as a written record, fixing relationships in print. The three most frequent literacy practices of the social queens (all considered out of bounds by the queens) were note-passing, writing graffiti, and reading teen zines— magazines marketed for adolescent consumption. In all their literacies, common themes emerged: Literacy is constructed as a social event with same-age peers, used to mark special status and allegiance, and also used to monitor and sustain social roles. Embracing the adolescent role received from the larger culture, the queens coopted sanctioned literate practices and engaged in literate underlife to document their opposition to adults by resisting institutional authority.

In all of the literate underlife, there existed a tremendous sense of play. Embedded within the play, the social queens used literacies for the following purposes: establishing a set of agreed-upon norms, competing for social status, connecting within a community, staking a claim, and defying authority. Clearly many literate behaviors supported more than one function, but all focused on the social aspects. Literate underlife, those literate practices that occur away from and in resistance to the institution of schooling, became a useful tool to mark status and document one as an insider in this group. Likewise, literate underlife was carefully monitored to keep outsiders out of the circle of friends. First I will discuss the literate underlife and then focus attention on the sanctioned practices of the social queens.

LITERATE UNDERLIFE

The social queens often asked me directly about the behaviors of other girls to assess how far out of bounds that social group might go. "What do they do that is bad?" was a recurring question, the word "bad" always emphasized with added volume and an elongated vowel sound. "Being bad" was a mark of status, a symbol of graduation from the "little girls" category to what the queens considered appropriate behaviors for "normal teenagers." The following list lifted from interview and classroom transcripts reflects the roles available for girls in the school context from the perspective of the queens:

woof-woofs	teenagers
babies	just regular girls
dogs	normal teenagers
little girls	
kids	

The labels on the left are different names for the same role: that of a girl who cannot meet the requirements of a normal teenager. Woof-woofs and dogs refer to the girls who were considered not physically attractive to boys. Little girls, babies, and kids refer to those who by virtue of their young age continue to follow rules. The queens, of course, considered themselves to be "just regular girls" or "normal teenagers," obliged by their credo to "be bad." Teenagers were those girls who were no longer children but now were defining themselves as young women. In contrast to dogs or woof-woofs, normal teenagers were physically attractive to males.

In describing what teachers expected, for example, Lauren's comment reveals her perceptions of appropriate roles for her: "They [teachers] expect us to be good all the time, but we are teenagers now." In an interview, Tiffany remarked, "They want us to act like little kids, but we're just acting like normal teenagers." The discourse of adolescence makes such roles available to these teens who from the larger culture have come to understand the role of the adolescent as the one who rebels. In dynamic interplay, the discourse creates the role and the enacted role perpetuates the discourse. From Tiffany's comment, we can infer that from the queens' perspective, what was appropriate behavior for children was no longer appropriate for teenagers. The queens perceived marked differences in their appropriate roles: Children are good. They do what they are told and follow rules. Teenagers, on the other hand, do not obey.

As sixth graders, these girls, by virtue of the school structure, were recognized as powerful because they were the oldest students in the building. They did not need to vie for status by proving their more adult status. Given opportunities for privilege—running errands, supervising smaller children—each queen's status was more secure. As junior high school began, however, the queens were the youngest, and thus had to earn a more adult status by enacting the role that for them marked them as adolescent. The shift in power forced these adolescents to establish new markers.

Yet, while Angie and Tiffany worked to enact their role as adolescents, they both had parents who supported the school authority and who demanded that their daughters respect teachers and achieve academically. The queens openly broke the rules to gain status among their peers; yet each calculated how far out-of-bounds she could go beyond the sanctions of school and safely remain in good standing at home.

Literacy events were a major site of struggle for this negotiation. Literate underlife created opportunities to disrupt the official, to document a refusal to embrace the obligations of the institution. Zine reading, note-passing, and writing on the rest-room walls served as acts of resistance against the institutional constructions of literacy while also creating strong bonds of solidarity among the girls.

Queens Reading the Zines

LAUREN: What do they [the "woof-woofs"] read? They probably just read books. They have nothing better to do.

ANGIE: They probably don't even read these [holds up a copy of Sassy].

TIFFANY: Did you guys see this? God, I'm gonna get some of these [holds open a page from YM and points to a pair of pants]. Isn't this so cool?

ANGIE: Way cool. My mom's gonna let me get some. Do you think I kinda look like her? [points to a model in Sassy]

LAUREN: Oh, yeah, right. Give me that. It's my copy. Give me that, you dork.

ANGIE: Give it to me. Who's the dork? Let me have it. Let me read you something.
TIFFANY: Know what? I'm gonna get *YM*. My dad said he'd loan me the money. He'll forget, and I won't have to pay him back.
ANGIE: Did you take this best friend quiz?
LAUREN: Did you see that article about who's in and who's out? I think he [TV star in zine] is so cool. He's a total babe. I mean B-A-B-E.

After one year of documenting the reading and writing practices of early adolescent females, I regularly came to expect scenes like this one, played out like a well-rehearsed script, girls turning to the pages of teen zines, seeking answers to questions about their place in an adolescent world. The social queens turned to the models for advice on their appearance and action. They denied adult presence and most often consumed these magazines hidden behind closed doors, far outside the judgmental gaze of significant adults. Teen zines were most often read in private places such as bedrooms and school rest rooms, places that might be considered safe havens away from adults and boys.

While, of course, adults produce these magazines, the girls perceived zines as exclusively their own, as out-of-bounds for adults. The girls never acknowledged any adult presence behind the youthful images, and most often considered the models to be the authors. When pushed by me to unpack the "They" that the early adolescents so often referred to in their talk about the magazines ("*They* tell you about boys and stuff," "*They* show you cool stuff," "*They* know what it's like to be a teenager today"), each focal student pointed to photographs of teens within the magazines, and each denied adult presence behind the text.

Girls in this social group reported with pride that their teachers and parents did not approve of such reading practices, making such comments as "She [mother] wants me to read books, but I read *Sassy*," "I put one [teen zine] in my notebook and read it during class, and Mr. T. doesn't even know it," "My mom doesn't like them. I hide them in my science folder." Those who carried zines were in a sense using literacy to make visible their entry into adolescence. Literacy served as an act of self-presentation. Not only were they documenting interest in what they considered adult content, but perhaps what is more important, they were demonstrating their defiance of adult authority by breaking the perceived rules of what constituted appropriate reading materials.

The presence of zines was used to document one's passage into adolescence, and zine absence was noted as well: "They probably don't even read these." Reading teen zines marks a boundary around one particular group of girls. The only girls who carried zines at school were the social queens. While the queens regularly reported reading and buying zines, the other girls denied reading them. Likewise, I saw no zines in their homes.

Lauren, one of the peer-reported "most popular" girls in the school, regularly referred to her friends as "normal teenagers" and as "regular teens" and often cited *Sassy* as a source of proof for appropriate teen dress and conduct. "See, this is cool," she reported, matching a magazine photograph of a pair of shorts with her own. Using teen zines as a way of borrowing authority, Lauren assessed her appearance and dress against the standards in the magazine. When Lauren asked, "What do they read?" (referring to Cleo and her friends), she made a distinction between friendship groups. From her perspective, zines were markers for teens who were no longer "girls" but now were defining themselves as young women. In contrast to appropriate girls' behavior to just "read books" because "they don't have anything better to do," teenagers, according to Lauren, were compelled by their newly acquired roles as adolescents to concern themselves with physical appearance and meeting zine standards of "cool."

Angie wondered of Cleo's group, "Don't they care what they look like? They look like little kids. God, they wouldn't even know what to do with stuff like this [points to fashions in a current zine]." The queens referred to those who did not read zines or adhere to their standards as "little kids" rather than "normal teenagers." Borrowing authority from the pages of the zines, the social queens measured status by the closeness of their match to zine fashions and used the zines to mark particular groups of early adolescent females as insiders.

Zine readings serve these adolescents at a very literal level. On the social-sexual journey toward adulthood, they provide signposts to document progress. Zine readings serve adolescents to unite particular groups of peers and exclude others, serving as a powerful tool to mark insiders and outsiders.

The following exchange between seventh-grade girls typifies conversations that surround the reading of teen zines.

ANGIE: Hey, did you guys know that . . . [She begins to read from *Sassy*, one of the most popular teen zines.]

LAUREN: Let me have that. [She pulls the magazine from Angie's grasp. Angie attempts to continue reading by shoving up against Lauren's shoulder.]

TIFFANY: That really pisses me off. Mine never comes first. [She rips the magazine out of her friend's hand. The girls laugh and wrestle over possession.]

ANGIE: Do you know what it's got? [Leaning across the library table, she grabs the magazine back, flips through the pages, searching for one article.] It's got this really gross article about sleeping with *your* stepdad.

LAUREN: God, that is gross. I wouldn't sleep with my stepdad. Can you even imagine you and Larry [Tiffany's stepfather]?

TIFFANY: Gross.

LAUREN: Gross.

After careful analysis of repeated occurrences of zine reading, three themes emerged from my data: (1) reading was an exclusive social event, (2) reading was used to assign special status, and (3) experiences reported in the magazines were appropriated by the girls as their own.

First, reading of these magazines was rarely a solitary act. In the broad cultural sense, the girls turned to zines to learn culturally specific ways of being a woman. One girl, for example, described her reason for reading teen zines in this way: "They tell you about woman stuff." What constituted "woman stuff" was mediated and negotiated through the reading of these magazines. Yet, within the pages themselves, there is a notable lack of adult images (Evans, Rutberg, Sather, & Turner, 1991). By concealing any adult presence, teen zines were embraced by early adolescent females as their own; yet the layout and content are orchestrated by marketers to make these young women into a particular kind of female. Teen zines transport a powerful economic ideology into the lives of these young women who are bathed in a set of societal norms for women. Teen zines echo the larger societal influences that constrict and enable particular gendered roles.

Beyond learning meaning in culturally appropriate ways, the social queens quite literally read in groups. Zine reading was fiercely social. Groups of girls crowded together on a bed, in a large recliner, or in the corner of the school library to devour the cherished possession and negotiate a unified front as to their collective opinion of each article and advertisement. Oftentimes, the arrival in the mail of a teen zine necessitated a "sleepover" to "hang together and look at our magazines." Social queens made arrangements to gather for this express purpose. These seventh-grade girls often bagged up back issues to cart to a Friday night slumber party.

I spent five hours at one such event. When I arrived at Angie's, her mother let me in and said, "Just follow the noise. They're already upstairs.'' I walked into Angie's bedroom, hair spray mist creating a perfumed fog, music and giggles vibrating the glossy teen photographs and celebrated designer labels that had been carefully removed from clothing or torn from the pages of teen zines and taped to the walls. Once I settled in on a corner of the bed, the girls quit screaming and resumed their activities. Angie returned to her position, curling and spraying Tiffany's long auburn locks in front of a full-length mirror that was framed with images of adolescent beauty, snapshots of friends juxtaposed with the latest models trimmed from the pages of *Sassy* and *Seventeen*. Beside me, Lauren continued to flip through the pages of a zine, offering a series of statements, ''This is cool,'' ''He is so cute,'' ''This dress is so totally awesome.'' Such statements were regularly interrupted with a question, ''Do you think he is cute?'' ''Do you think that's cool?'' ''Do you think she's pretty?'' After each question, usually delivered with a tone that conveyed an assumed answer, Tiffany and Angie would turn from the mirror to glance momentarily at the picture in question and then together would answer, ''Yeah'' or ''Not.''

It was almost always a mutual agreement. The girls rarely disagreed and, when they did, they argued until a consensus was reached. Someone would have to give up on her opinion. Someone always did. No page was turned until the girls all agreed about fashion or face, beauty or body.

According to Goffman (1959), individuals on a team work together backstage in order to present a unified front when they are on center stage. Scenes like this one, played out in the girls' bedrooms and in the school rest rooms, match what Goffman described as backstage rehearsals for their more public performances.

On this particular Friday night, these early adolescents were practicing their adult roles, rehearsing their opinions with the help of a carefully constructed script, the teen zine. Also, in backstage regions, the queens used zines to check and test ways of being adolescent. Those who were deemed in need of remediation were schooled by the others with the zine serving as an authoritative textbook. Queens made such remarks as, ''Dah, you are so stupid. Look at this [pointing to a page in *Sassy*]'' and ''Jes, you should wear your hair like this [pointing to a page in *YM*].''

At this developmental period, while much may have appeared unstable, zines provided solid guidelines. The girls often reported, ''See, it shows you what's cool.'' At a time when all rules and rituals appear to be in flux, when even her body forsakes her, the early adolescent can turn to the pages of a teen zine for firm control. This illusion of stability provides a sense of power and control in a world that is often perceived as out of control. As these girls entered the new social arena of adolescence, zines served as a handbook.

Second, the girls used teen zines to assign special status. At a literal level, there appeared to be two dimensions of status building: being the first to possess the latest issue of a zine and, more importantly, being the owner of that copy. Note Tiffany's comment, "That really pisses me off. Mine never comes first." Copies borrowed from a friend or the library carried much less clout. When a magazine was borrowed, one could not control the circulation as readily, and one could not control distribution of individual pages. The girl who arrived at school or at a slumber party first with the latest issue of a teen zine tucked under her arm wielded more power and prestige, controlling circulation of the latest important information about fashion, beauty, and entertainment.

When a magazine arrived, these girls rushed to obtain the coveted position of being first by calling a best friend before the cover of the magazine had even been opened. As the phone was ringing, one hurried to find an article worthy of reading into the receiver in order to prove that one was indeed first. Being first merited clout because one's name became attached to the latest information. Comments such as "Lauren says that there is this awesome fingernail polish in *YM*," and "Lauren says that the Mall of America is bigger than a bunch of football fields" circulated around the junior high.

On another level, status was achieved by possessing the closest match to the fashions and appearances transported by the teens in the text. Although Angie had been the envy of two of her best friends since she began subscribing to *Sassy* in the middle of her sixth-grade year, she did not hold the powerful position of director. It's hardly surprising that that role was assigned to Lauren, who was claimed by all as "the prettiest" with "the best bod," and "she's the one with the most boyfriends." In other words, Lauren's physical features represented the closest match to those present on the pages of any zine. As director, Lauren regularly orchestrated the actions and opinions of the other girls. So whenever the girls got together to negotiate their collective opinions, Lauren most often held the magazine and held the final word.

Girls appropriated the experiences reported in the articles as their own. Just as Angie said "sleeping with *your* stepdad," Lauren and Tiffany regularly used the pronouns "you" and "your" and directly made claims that the young women in the advertisements and articles were "just like me." In interviews, they said such things as "It [*Sassy*] tells the most embarrassing things of *your* life," and "See, it [*YM* magazine] shows *you* what is cool," and "I read it [*Sassy*] because I want to know about AIDS and stuff, and I want to know what happens to girls *just like me.''* In some ways the teens in the zines were just like them. A content analysis of the three top-selling teen magazines revealed those zines were populated in the following manner: Euro-American females 65.2%, Euro-American males 24.5%, Non-Euro-American females 7.7%, and Non-Euro-American males 2.6%, with adults of any color rare and limited to the even more rare educational career article (Evans et al., 1991, p. 109).

A strong sense of community bridged from those present in the text to those present in the immediate context. The queens talked about the articles as if each carried an implicit command that one must follow in order to achieve high status. Their talk implied a powerful connectedness to the teens in the magazines. Following is one such incident in which the conversation weaves in and out from text to immediate bedroom scene, lacing them together in the present:

ANGIE: So what did Ronnie say about me?
LAUREN: He said that you are fine. He goes, ''She's a babe.''
TIFFANY: Come on, Lauren.
ANGIE: You know what? I just broke out in zits majorly.
TIFFANY: Me too. It must be zit week or something.
LAUREN: I know, I look in the mirror and God. Did you take this kissing quiz? [Reference to a quiz in one of the teen zines]
TIFFANY: I was giving Sara the quiz on the phone. Do you have any sweats?
ANGIE: I don't have any sweats. I got some stretch pants you can wear.
TIFFANY: Dang, this curling iron doesn't even work.
LAUREN: Maybe I should get some of these [reference to jeans in advertisement]. When I get older, I'm gonna get braces so my teeth will look like this [points to model in teen zine].
ANGIE: I want to try on those colored pocket pants of yours. Can I?
LAUREN: Do it. Ouch! Watch where you sit.
TIFFANY: Okay, here's this thing. [She begins reading from a zine.] ''As my boy friend and I are leaving my house to go to the game, my little sister had to come along [breaks into laughter, inaudible] and she asks me why I had put so many tissues in my bra.''

The invisibility of adults and the strong sense of sameness may have fostered a sense of seamless connection between their friends and experiences and those in the zines. Zines were often held up almost like a mirror and used, it seems, to reinforce cultural standards of adolescent beauty. Just as Willinsky and Hunniford (1993) argue that books provide mirrors for early adolescents, the social queens often pointed to teen zines and asked, "Do you think I look like her?" "Do you think my hair looks like this?" "Do you think these jeans would look good on me?" Lacking a critical distance that fiction creates, zines were received as truths; the girls often quite literally lifted phrases directly from the pages to become part of their language. As Bakhtin (1981) suggests, their words come out of other people's mouths.

One appropriates another's voice as a means of borrowing authority (Shuman, 1993, p. 136). Descriptions of their best friends seem to borrow authority from zine models. Such descriptions contained not only the rhythms and constructions but often the exact words that fill the texts of the teen zines: "She has her thick, dark, luxurious hair that you could die for and beautiful sky blue eyes." "She has a perfect creamy complexion and a perfect posture." In separate interviews, when asked to describe a best friend, the word "perfect" emerged in seven out of eight interviews and was repeated at least twice in three. I was struck by the emphasis on perfection, on the singular standard that is so well established that a 13-year-old is marked because her hips are already "too wide" by an agreed-on cultural standard that celebrates slimness.

In December of their seventh grade year, Tiffany reported that she was "finally allowed to spend my own Christmas money to get *Sassy*." She had succeeded, in her own words, "by ragging my mom for about a year." Their disagreements over teen magazines became clear during my first visit to their home:

M.F.: What else do you read? Do you read any magazines?

TIFFANY: *YM* [She giggles and looks at her mother out of the corner of her eye.]

M.F.: Do you get that at home?

TIFFANY: I don't get them, but I get them at the library. [She turns to plead for her mother to buy the magazine for her.] But, Mom, get them. That's what I read.

MOTHER [laughs and reaches over to the magazine rack to pick up a copy of *YM*]: I'm not really comfortable with these teen magazines.

TIFFANY: Mom!

MOTHER: She likes to read trash.

TIFFANY: Yep!

MOTHER: Well, the advertisements are just too sensual.

TIFFANY [taking the copy from her mother, she slowly turns the pages, scrutinizing each one]: What advertisements?

MOTHER: Maybe when she gets older she can get those magazines. I can't think that that reading experience will *broaden* your horizons.

[Her sarcastic tone and glance are directed toward Tiffany. She turns back to me.] But she *is* reading.

One can sense the tensions in this parent. On the one hand she did not want her daughter to be exposed to such "sensual" materials, but, on the other hand, she acknowledged that such contents motivated her daughter's reading. She explained further about her daughter's time spent reading *YM*: "I know it's not wasted. It's still reading but it's like fluff." Later in the conversation, this parent admitted that she, like her daughter, often enjoyed what she called "reading fluff." She said, "I do a lot of studying now, and I think I've got to find something that's just that [fluff]. When I pick something up, a *McCall's* or a newsstand-type magazine and read those things, you don't have to think about it. I suppose that's very similar to what you do, Tiff."

Clearly, Tiffany's reading was very similar to her mother's account of reading as "fluff." What was missed in this discussion of "fluff reading" was Tiffany's misreading of the advertisements. In magazines that according to Evans and colleagues (1991) give 46% of their total space over to advertisements, it might seem remarkable that Tiffany was blind to it. On the following day at school, I asked Tiffany to explain about the advertisements in the magazines. She insisted, "There aren't any ads." She proceeded to prove it to me. Pulling the latest issue of *Sassy* from her notebook, turning from ads to articles through full- and half-page ads, she argued, "This tells you about fingernail polish. This shows you about makeup. This is about zits and stuff. See?"

Tiffany's emphasis on "See?" illustrates her use of these magazines as a kind of proof. She trusted the editors to do exactly what those at *Seventeen* had promised, "to provide her with all of the information she needed to make sound choices" (Peirce, 1990, pp. 496–497). The seduction of these magazines is powerful. While it may appear that Tiffany was just extremely naive, the layout of teen zines is, in fact, quite seductive. Articles and advertisements look remarkably alike. Articles often are presented as whole-page photos with a column on the left that details the dress complete with designer names and suggested retail prices. The girls demonstrate little ability to consciously grasp such an economic ideology. The comment "What advertisements?" illustrates dramatically how these teens are lulled into accepting such a constrictive economic package.

The social queens used the articles and advertisements alike as criteria for establishing their own social roles and for judging those of others. They pointed to the models in the pages to ask, "Am I fatter than her?"

"Would that look good on me?" "Do you think that's cool?" "Do I look like her?" Thus they rehearsed their values and opinions with the assistance of these magazines marketed specifically for them. They measured their friends and foes alike by the singular standard that permeates the pages of *YM*, *Sassy*, *Teen*, and *Seventeen*.

When one observes how readily these girls appropriate the words, experiences, and images of the magazines as their own, one can hardly deny the impact of these texts on the social construction of self. These teens accepted such images as a ruler by which adolescent girls measure their own successes as they try on more adult roles. Such messages, while quite overt to critical scholars, remain invisible to these young women. Behind closed doors, these girls were left to their own devices to interpret, integrate, and mediate the images and text. These messages read over and over became scripts for the girls.

Note-passing: Struggles for Status

Note-writing as a genre did not allow for much individual expression or originality. The girls all protested indignantly whenever I suggested such a notion: "You can write whatever you want." Yet, the following notes illustrate the standards required for the genre of note-writing.

> Lauren,
> Yo! What's up? Not much here. I'm in math and it is BORING. Did you know that I like Nate alot. But he'd probably never go out with me caz I'm too ugly. AND FAT. Oh, well though. I'm still going to try and get him to go with me caz I like him. I hope he goes with me before the football game Friday. I want to be going with him at the game. Are you and Ricky going to the game? I want to go somewhere after that. Maybe you could come over or I could come to your house. Don't show this to anyone. W-B [Write Back] Maggie

> Lauren,
> Hey, What's up? You don't need to ask Bill for me cause he won't go and he's just that way I guess. You can try but I know he's not going to go. Well I'm almost positive. I'm in social studies and I just got busted caz I had none of my homework done. Fun. My handwriting majorly Sucks. I hate it. Go to *Body Guard* at the mall and I'll say you need a ride home. Then you can spend the night at my house. Call me tonight. I will be at my mom's. S.S. [Stay Sweet or Stay Sexy] Carrie.

Notes regularly began with a common salutation, "Hey, what's up?" followed by a reference to where the note was written—"I'm in math." "I'm in social studies." Because notes were always written in school, this move positioned the queen in opposition to the institutional power by boldly announcing an act of defiance during one particular class and then adding a condemning judgment such as, "It's so boring." In this move, queens perceived themselves as powerful by defying authority. Yet, that power was somewhat diffused as they often embedded in the body of the note a reference to themselves as inadequate: too fat, too ugly, my handwriting sucks. Often in notes, messages closed with "Sorry So Sloppy," which were sometimes shortened to S.S.S. For the most part, extreme care was taken to write neatly, at times dotting the i's with circles or hearts.

The content of notes was generally about making social arrangements for after-school activities and for requesting help in making romantic contacts. The notes carried highly coded messages such as N.M.H. [not much here] that limited the readership to those who were inside the circle of friends. The closing, as well, was most often highly coded—B.F.F. [best friends forever] W-B [write back]—to provide an insider quality to those who knew the codes. Britton (1970), noting the "with-it" language of adolescents, argues for the necessity of "drawing together members of a group or the set, and keeping outsiders out" (p. 235). The meaning behind S.S.S. evolved over time. At first it meant "Sorry So Sloppy," but over the course of the seventh-grade year, it came to carry a completely different meaning: "Stay Sweet and Sexy." The evolution of this one code illustrates the demands embedded within shifting social roles from girl to adolescent.

Although notes generally followed a standard format, a few did contain important unknown information such as the appropriate time to receive a call, an apology for flirting with a boyfriend, or guarded information about family problems. The queens attempted to control the circulation of their notes and regularly added to their messages, "Don't show this to anyone." For the most part, notes created boundaries around a group of friends. By creating a tangible document, girls created proof of their memberships.

As stated previously, girls all voiced the opinion that "you just write whatever you want," yet, when someone outside the intimate circle of friends wrote a note to one of the most popular girls, she was criticized. As one girl described it, "Look at that. She doesn't even know how to write right." These teens were criticized for not recognizing or following the rules and rituals of note-writing, a primary rule being that notes could be passed only to friends of equal social status.

The unstated rules of adhering to established social hierarchies were clearly enforced. If, for example, a girl did not know her place in the social hierarchy and wrote a note to a more popular girl, she became the object of ridicule and laughter within the higher circle.

This need for social sorting at the junior high was visible to teachers. Debra Zmoleck described the practice in this way:

> I think part of the way junior high kids feel good about themselves is they've got to have that ego, you know, it's a pecking order. They've got to have somebody that's down there that all the other chickens peck at, you know. And I don't know why. I guess it's just part of junior high.

The "pecking order" to which Debra referred was often documented in literate practices. Literacy was a tool used to document and maintain social position. In private interviews, Angie and Lauren both made statements in accord with Tiffany's own self-assessment:

> I don't write notes much so now I don't get 'em. Lauren gets the most because she writes the most. She's the most popular. Me, not so much.

Tiffany lost status because she didn't write as many notes as other girls and slowly over time received fewer and fewer, marking her as less popular. On the other hand, Lauren was perceived to be the most popular girl among her network of friends because "she has the most notes." She also received more notes from boys, which further served to document her high status among her friends.

In the fall of seventh grade, the number of notes passed increased until mid-November when a plateau was reached; January saw a sharp decline. When asked about this decline, the queens all relayed the fact that there just wasn't as much to write about; yet the events that they had written about all year—social arrangements, sports, and boys—had not decreased in their interest or in their activity. I contend that note-passing had served its purpose—to sort and select a hierarchy among the queens who had just entered a new arena in the fall. Arriving from different sixth-grade classrooms, the queens used literacies in the new school context to negotiate entry into new friendship networks. Through print sources, they maintained familiar ties in this strange new world, connecting at first with old sixth-grade friends and then negotiating their ways into other social groups. By January, new social positions were securely established, and note-passing decreased because jockeying for position was no longer an option for gaining status or entry into the social queens' network.

Note-passing was clearly a gendered activity. It functioned to control male voices and to try out women's voices. Circulation of notes was controlled exclusively by girls. Girls decided who was entitled to see, receive, or write a note. Boys did not write notes to boys, and they wrote to girls only when they were invited or instructed to do so by a girl directly or through a channeling system, where one girl wrote to another girl who would then write to a boy, thereby granting him permission to write to the first girl. This act of literacy bestowed power and control of romantic interactions exclusively to females. The hierarchical arrangement placed power firmly in the hands of the social queens, who controlled and regulated which boys wrote or received notes.

To guard the circulation of messages, the queens informed me that learning to fold a note properly was vital to ensure that it would not open if it are dropped. Notes were folded into small triangles or squares with edges tucked in, serving as a lock to protect messages from unauthorized eyes. Such skill in intricate folding was also used to gain status within the inner circle. One's knowledge of elaborate folds signaled one as a member in good standing. Again, literacy served to document status within this circle of friends. If one queen learned a new and extremely complex fold, she received high praise and then attained the honored position of teacher, instructing others in how to fold.

Note-folding was a crucial skill because passing the note was a fine game that required a small, streamlined object. A note could have no rough edges to catch in a pocket lining, and it must be easily manipulated in the palm of one hand in order to avoid detection as it slipped from hand to hand boldly under the nose of a teacher. Passing notes from one of the social queens to another under the sharp scrutiny of a teacher was seen by these girls as an act of defiance and a behavior to be admired. Girls wrote, circulated, and responded to notes while reading aloud, participating in classroom discussions, and completing written work. A girl, for instance, could participate in a large-group discussion while writing and then passing notes without skipping a beat as she actively engaged in the classroom discussion. Designed to fool the teacher into thinking one was paying attention, such a game documented allegiance to peers. Ironically, a queen had to pay extremely close attention to keep the game going in her favor; yet this game was played to make the teacher appear foolish and the teen powerful.

Whenever the risk became heightened by a teacher's reprimands or threats of posting notes on classroom walls, notes became a greater avenue of status-building. When the risk were greatest, girls began lacing their texts with obscene language to up the ante, for to have one such note confiscated would mean not only a disruption at school but disruption at home as well.

More often than not, the content of the note was inconsequential; meaning was conveyed in the passing of the note rather than within the text itself. The act of passing the note during class relayed the message, an act of defiance of adult authority. The message was modified not through words but through the creative manipulation of the passing. The closer one was to the teacher physically when the note was written or delivered, the more powerful the message. By mid-November, after the girls had grown to trust me, they would often dig into their pockets and notebooks and hand me unopened notes. They did not need to read the notes because the message was implicit in the process of passing: in clues such as who sent, who received, who was present during the passing, and how the note was transported.

After I examined note-passing as a ritualized event, several themes emerged: (1) Writing is a social event; (2) special status is ascribed to the girl who received the most notes, especially from boys; and (3) meaning often resides in the act of passing a note. Note-passing was a tool used to document and maintain social position. For the most part, notes were used to bestow power and patrol boundaries around a group of friends.

Graffiti: Staking a Claim

Like note-passing, graffiti writing documented social positions. After several months of collecting graffiti from the school rest-room walls, the contents of which were generally sexual in nature, I casually asked, "Do you ever read any of that stuff written in the bathroom?" Without pause, Angie, Lauren, and Tiffany exclaimed, "Read it? We write it!" They proudly proclaimed ownership of some of the rest-room texts. They immediately took me to the rest room to point out their work: "Nan and Leslie are lessies," "Nathan R. has no balls," "Mr. Anson is a fagget [sic]." While these girls willingly accepted ownership of the written texts on the walls, they never spoke such words in my presence.

The social queens were writing for their peers, in the privacy of the rest room, an exclusive literacy club, a safe haven away from adults and boys. The texts were filled with sexual confusion; issues of sexual orientation, promiscuity, and body functions were tested here.

The girls' rest room can best be understood as one of the few private spaces in the public arena of school, a "backstage region." In the sanctuary of the rest room, Tiffany, Angie, and Lauren were rehearsing their adult roles, their adult voices; yet the words were not yet their own. Messages about women received from the larger culture were tested and tried.

While the rest room may be a region away from boys and adults, it appeared that the queens still used the arena to perform for each other, vying for status and recognition. With red blotches creeping up her neck, eyes downcast, voice quivering, Angie seemed ill at ease with this particular writing practice, yet she openly admitted that she did write boys' names. Tiffany, on the other hand, leaping to the toilet seat, stretching up, pen in hand, wrote on the ceiling boldly in my presence, sustaining her self-proclaimed role as the most rebellious of the group. Consciously and deliberately the queens used print to not only document their roles as normal, rule-breaking teenagers, but here, they wrote to create a physical distance, which, as Britton (1970) suggests, "allows a writer, if he [she] needs to, to wrestle with his [her] thoughts, to work and re-work his [her] formulation of projection or transformation of experience" (p. 248).

Graffiti served these girls to work and rework their roles as women. The following reveals the level of overt awareness as to the function of this activity:

M.F.: Do you really write on the wall in there?

ANGIE: Yep.

M.F.: Why?

ANGIE: Cause if you write a boy's name in there then nobody else can. It's sort of proof.

M.F.: Proof? What kind of proof?

ANGIE: Like, if you like a guy and you write his name in there, then nobody else can like him.

LAUREN: Yeah, like if you don't like him any more, you cross out his name, and then he's fair game.

M.F.: So if I liked some guy and I wrote like, "I love Jim," than Tiffany couldn't like him.

LAUREN: Unless you said she could. She'd have to ask you.

TIFFANY [laughing]: Remember when we wrote in the boys' bathroom. We wrote Lauren's phone number for a good time.

M.F.: What about all of that other stuff in there? Not just about liking boys?

LAUREN: We write it to make somebody mad. Like I wrote Erin Barton's big [She laughs and censors herself] you-know-what. And somebody wrote Lauren is a F'n bitch and stuff like that.

Graffiti writing served these girls to document their claims over particular boys and again to exercise their power in a world that for the most part was beyond their control. Graffiti writing as "proof" served as official documentation, securing relationships in print. Relationships locked into print could not be disputed.

Considering themselves to be young women, the queens used literacy to gain control over this new position. Messages were almost exclusively sexual in nature. Messages pushed the boundaries into the forbidden. As an act of resistance, such writing provided power over institutional constraints. Graffiti writing was documented "proof" of their control over boys, their control over their own sexuality, and their control over institutional authority.

Although writing served as a record to document relationships, shifting relationships demanded revision. Girls made arrangements to meet at a particular time in a particular rest room to read and revise the walls. Two days after "Shawn Loves Erin Barton" appeared, a "Not" appeared beneath the phrase. Messages were added to, scribbled out, and answered. In the school setting, the girls' rest room provided the only backstage area in the school; off-limits to boys and rarely visited by adults, this sanctuary was a literacy haven in which girls proclaimed, challenged, investigated, and negotiated their adolescent roles.

SCHOOL-SANCTIONED LITERACIES

The social queens met school-sanctioned literacies with much less passion, interest, or enthusiasm. For them, the rules within the institution were understood implicitly as rules for younger girls to follow. Documenting an allegiance to their friends, they concealed any connectedness they may have felt with adults within the school context. When asked, "What do you think influences your book selections most?" Angie answered:

> Tiffany. Like in fifth grade I never read at all. Me and Lauren are like best friends, and she didn't read, so I didn't read. But sixth grade, I got to know Tiffany really well, and she always read, and she is always telling me about these good books, like everything that happens, and then I went out and bought some books, and I'd read them, and she'd read, and we both read the same books and talked about them and everything.

It might appear that these girls would be successful in the language arts classroom because they so highly prize the social aspects of learning. Their attitudes and those of their parents closely matched those within the institution. On the one hand, this practice of sharing texts was something most language arts teachers would highly value. Likewise, these girls all reported that group work and group projects were extremely enjoyable. On the other hand, their allegiance to their peers often interfered with any intellectual engagement. Because their social roles were so tied to the expectations brought to the classroom by their peers, these girls often staged performances that worked against any sanctioned literacy instruction.

They completed most language arts assignments with little regard for the quality of their work. In fact, for the most part it appeared that the social queens understood classroom literacy instruction in only the most superficial ways. When asked to elaborate on what criteria were used for evaluation in language arts, Angie explained:

> He doesn't do too much grading, but like sometimes he'll walk around, and if somebody has the date on their paper he'll give five extra points, but there's not too much grading in there.

Academic drive was external. Most often it was built on threats of being grounded at home. The queens dutifully completed assignments so they wouldn't get in trouble and immobilized at home. Intellectual rigor, curiosity, or engagement were minimal. On those rare occasions in which a queen became intrigued with any language arts project or assignment, she attempted to conceal it. Having worked so hard to establish a social position within her friendship circle, each queen attempted to maintain her role, refusing to threaten her position within that social network. On multiple occasions, the queens described their roles in the following manner:

ANGIE: Lauren's the flirtatious one. Tiffany is the red-headed one.
    I'm the one that does my homework.
TIFFANY: Yeah, she's the one that does her homework, and she lets
    us have it.

Angie, it seemed, had been cast into the role of "good student." Her friends defined her as "the one who does her homework and always wants to get an A." Angie did want to earn As, but she also wanted to know what the minimum was for an A, and she wanted to maintain her role as teenager within the social network. The following transcript reflects Angie's ability to sustain two somewhat competing roles, protecting her role as a good student while coopting school sanctions:

M.F.: What makes a story good?
TIFFANY: I liked your story, Angie.
M.F.: What is it about Angie's story that you liked?
TIFFANY: It was interesting.
M.F.: What made it interesting?
TIFFANY: I don't remember. Angie, give me a short little refresher. What was yours about?
ANGIE: I don't know. I don't like my story.
M.F.: When did you hand it in?
ANGIE: Yesterday.
TIFFANY [laughs]: It is supposed to be Tuesday, but mine was late.
M.F.: Can you remember what yours is about?
TIFFANY: No! [laughs and directs the question to Angie] Do you?
ANGIE: Yeah. [to me] She paid me $3.00 to write it for her.
TIFFANY: Yeah, but I finished it.

In this interview, both Tiffany and Angie denied engagement with sanctioned literacy instruction. It is highly doubtful that neither could remember what she had written or turned in on the preceding day; yet for me, for each other, and for themselves they showcased this disengagement.

Maintaining similar constructions of school-sanctioned practices, the queens all wanted to know what the teacher's minimum expectations were, what they could get away with, what they would get for good work. They did the least required. Assignments were often circulated among the queens. Queens borrowed and bought right answers to avoid "wasting their time." Angie and Carrie, who carried the designation of "good students," often loaned or sold essays and short stories to others in order to work against the institutional sanctions while still maintaining their connection to these sanctions.

Tiffany was regularly described as "the red-head." Such a distinguishing mark had cast her into the role of a boisterous rebel, which carried with it an implicit charge to boldly defy adult authority. Just as Angie worked to support her reputation as an A student, Tiffany concealed any connection she felt with adults in authority. The following examples illustrate how successful she was at concealing her engagement with literature.

Tiffany was tardy (or almost tardy) to her language arts class more often than not. Flying into the room, slamming her books on her desk at the front of the room where Mr. Tibidioux assigned her to sit in an attempt to control her talking and disruptive behavior, Tiffany boldly announced her arrival. Then, mocking the role of a good student, she often insisted that she needed to go to her locker to get her books because she had been so conscientious to arrive before the tardy bell that she simply had not had time to stop at her locker in preparation for this class.

Mr. Tibidioux came to expect the disruption of Tiffany's arrival scene. For Tiffany, the repetition of the scene created an opportunity to perform for her peers. Her assigned seat at the front was a stage from which Tiffany powerfully coopted the literacy lesson, delaying the beginning of the lesson for one or two minutes for the enjoyment of her peers. Her dislike for language arts class and especially for Mr. Tibidioux, her teacher, were well known. Her parents worried about it. Her friends laughed at it. Mr. Tibidioux ignored all but the worst of her behaviors and highly praised any glimpse of engagement that he noticed.

Her autobiography, "The Creation of Big Red," held a prominent position in Mr. Tibidioux's classroom, displayed in the center of the student bulletin board with generous comments of teacherly praise written in the margins throughout the text. In an attempt to connect with Tiffany, Mr. Tibidioux lavishly praised the very thing he knew she valued most, her role as troublemaker. Following are two excerpts from "The Creation of Big Red" with Mr. Tibidioux's written comments in italics:

> When I was in my terrible twos, I was a pain in the butt. While my mom was cleaning up one mess, I would be making another mess. Instead of coloring a little bit on the walls, I would color big murals. *Fantastic Detail. You tell us how, you show us!*

> At ten we moved to a house on South Lawn Drive. My mom and Larry got married, and I started fourth grade at Woods. I got out of fourth grade that summer, and met a girl named Lauren. We hung out the whole summer and got in trouble a lot. We became best friends that summer. *You introduce an important person here.*

At the bottom of the paper were written the following teacher comments:

> Tiffany, I'm impressed by your goals and the clarity of this paper. You clearly described your life. I'm so excited to see how much you

enjoyed this assignment. You worked hard at writing about *What Matters Most*. Nice work. A

Secretly, this pleased Tiffany. She told me privately in my exit interview that her autobiography was the best piece she had ever written, but publicly she mocked Mr. Tibidioux's approval and announced to her classmates that she had spent no time at all on it and that her mother had, in fact, typed it for her. Constricted by the role she maintained, Tiffany would not publicly acknowledge any pride in this piece of writing.

Near the end of the year, Mr. Tibidioux read *The Cay* by Theodore Taylor aloud to his seventh-period class. Again, Tiffany mocked his practice. In class, she pretended not to listen. With her head resting on her desk, she scowled and yawned. She closed her eyes. Her quiz scores documented that she had paid little attention; yet, in the privacy of an interview, she vividly recounted minute details of the book. The book had captivated her. She related selected scenes to her life experience. She connected the reading to other books that she had read; yet her public performances denounced this "baby book."

MR. TIBIDIOUX: Tiffany, how do you like *The Cay* so far?
TIFFANY: It's boring. I don't like adventures.
MR. TIBIDIOUX: Can you review for the rest of the class, what happened yesterday?
TIFFANY: Huh? I don't. I don't know. It was boring.

In a private interview the following day, Tiffany sought to sustain her role:

M.F.: How is it going in language arts?
TIFFANY: Scooby-do is reading to us. He thinks we are babies. He just reads aloud for almost the whole period. It is so boring.
M.F.: Do you like *The Cay* so far?
TIFFANY: No. I want to change classes, but he won't let me.
M.F.: What is *The Cay* about?
TIFFANY: I don't know. I didn't read the first chapter.
M.F.: Tiffany, I know you read it.
TIFFANY: Okay, Okay. There was this boy Phillip. His mom and his dad got in a fight. It was an argument. And the best part—she decided to leave and they got on this boat and it went on fire and um and so they put the people on rafts and Phillip and his mother
. . . [gives a detailed account of the main characters, Phillip and

Timothy. She continues] Timothy jumped in and grabbed Phillip when he fell in the water. All of the sudden Phillip got on the raft and started yelling. Timothy was still in the water. And then Timothy started yelling "Shark, Shark" [changes inflection in an attempt to match the accent of Timothy, as portrayed by her teacher on the previous day]. So he jumped up on the boat and started yelling. "You know, young boss, you could die like that. Never, never do that again. Young boss. Young boss" [switches back to her accent] like that. Like that.

Neither Mr. Tibidioux nor her classmates were allowed to view her enthusiasm or catch a glimmer of the impact that the book was having on her. Her journal responses, essays, and quiz scores confirmed Mr. Tibidioux's year-long observations and supported his assessment that Tiffany was a nonmotivated, average-ability reader.

Teachers who did not have Tiffany in class knew her as "that loud, red-headed girl." Her reputation as a rebel reduced her to this single dimension. At the end of the school year, I shared some of my findings with the language arts staff. Teachers perceived Tiffany as a average-level student and a nonreader. When I described Tiffany as an avid pleasure reader, teachers expressed doubt. Mrs. Zmoleck registered shock on hearing my account of Tiffany's home reading practices of regularly spending 45 minutes to an hour reading each night. The list of 44 books that Tiffany had checked out from the junior high library along with Tiffany's mother's description of one of Tiffany's evening rituals of climbing into a tub of hot water and reading a mystery until the water became too cold were more than surprising to Mrs. Zmoleck. She acknowledged with astonishment that she had something in common with Tiffany: "I do that too." She went on:

I can't believe she would read *anything*. Every day she's running in the hall with a malt. [It is against school policy to leave the lunch room with food.] Yesterday, she was trying to get Mr. Anson [the principal] to write her a pass to class so she could finish her malt. She's always tardy. I can't believe *she's* a reader.

Before any of these teachers is accused of reductive thinking, it must be reiterated that Tiffany worked very hard to conceal the fact that she was a reader and worked equally hard to construct an image of herself as an uninterested learner. Her school performances effectively conveyed one particular type of role—one that privileged the impressions and opinions of her peers over any adult.

Her tardiness was acknowledged among the friendship network as a way to "Get Mr. Tibidioux," a game she enjoyed playing at every opportunity. Similar games played by adolescents to slow down teaching and entertain peers are documented in other studies of adolescents (see, for example, Everhart, 1983; and Foley, 1990). "Kissing up" was a common game played by Tiffany and all of the social queens.

Kissing up consisted of a variety of teacher-pleasing practices. The kissing-up routine took on many forms and emerged in many facets—from a polite hello in the hallway to a face-to-face lie about the time spent on a project. "Mr. T., that's a fine shirt," "Can I pass out the folders?" "I'll read first," are three common examples. At times such expressions carried a thick sugar coating, making both teacher and students keenly aware of the performative nature of the act, mocking the practice. At other times, kissing up was disguised as a cheerful greeting in the hallway or an enthusiastic request to read aloud in class. Any feigning of engagement with the lessons was a part of the kissing-up game.

Perceived as the only way to get good grades and avoid reprimands at home, kissing up was perceived as the easiest way to succeed within the sanctioned literacy practices and save face within the peer network. The social queens needed to succeed in class to avoid losing privileges at home; playing the kissing-up game allowed a queen to engage in some literacy learning while protecting her position within peer networks. Tiffany and Angie both acknowledged kissing up as the key to school success:

M.F.: How would you describe yourselves in class and out of class?
ANGIE: In class I kiss up to the teachers and out of class, I don't kiss up to my friends.
M.F. [To Tiffany]: Would you agree with that? I think you said the very same thing. You used the same words. You said you have to kiss up to teachers.
TIFFANY: You have to. You have to kiss up.
ANGIE: You do. They have nothing to grade you on except for how much you kiss up.

Kissing up was considered to be the one and only way to succeed, something that must be done in order to get good grades and ultimately appease parents. It was a game played at a very conscious level, used to directly manipulate teachers but also used to save face when a queen might be accused of intellectual engagement. On occasion, a student's seemingly sincere interactions were later carefully dismissed with a

"Did you see me kiss Scooby-doo's butt in there today? I was really kissing up today."

The girls in the popular crowd for the most part tried to avoid anything that might be even remotely sanctioned in the classroom. As seventh graders, their performances must deny engagement; even Angie, who prided herself in getting straight As, most often made light of that fact and wanted to be seen as a straight-A student who did not really care.

Caring about learning was considered a sign of weakness, a mark of being a little girl who still needed to align herself with significant adults. For example, as sixth graders, the queens purchased books from the book clubs. In seventh grade, however, while the girls often accepted book club handouts and thumbed through them during class, they quickly discarded them into the wastebasket as the bell rang. Rather than "buy" into anything that the school promoted, these girls wanted to be seen as rebels, as students who refused to play by the "rules."

In order to present a unified front, queens staged performances to deny intellectual engagement. Along with kissing up, another routine was the regular "Leave your book in your locker" game, designed to gain power because it carries the privilege of added mobility, allowing one to leave the room and at times meet a friend in the rest room. Lauren explained, "I just tell them I'm sick or I left something in my locker then I hang out in here [the rest room]." Tiffany reported that she requested permission to go to her locker in order to meet Lauren, who was in another language arts class. Such routines were intended to convey the message to peers that one was not the least bit engaged in learning.

A consequence of such "team membership" was that the social queens refused to disrupt their unified front. Adhering to a rigid set of rules established by the group, queens were constrained to a limited set of patterned behaviors. An example of this was overtly visible in the texts that queens carried with them. These girls all carried the same kinds of books: At this time it was R. L. Stine and Christopher Pike novels. No other novels were seen being carried in the stacks of textbooks and notebooks, although the library computerized checkout system revealed that a much wider range of materials was, in fact, checked out regularly by these girls. Books such as baseball record books and those from the Baby Sitter's Club series were checked out, but they did not find their way into the language arts classroom.

Lauren, like Tiffany, embraced the role of rebel. To protect her image, she did not carry a novel to language arts class, choosing instead to just grab one off the shelf in the classroom. This performance, like

Tiffany's, was staged to present a particular kind of self to her class-mates. Like Mr. Tibidioux, Lauren's language arts teacher was surprised to learn that she checked out books such as *Baseball Record Book, The Complete Handbook of Baseball, Baseball Super Stats, Basketball All Stars, Everything You Need to Know about AIDS*, and *Ryan White: My Own Story*. None of those books appeared on her reading record, and her language arts teacher had not seen any during class. Clearly, sports books did not carry currency with the queens, and Lauren felt compelled to conceal her interest in athletics. Of the 39 books that Lauren had checked out of the junior high library (21 of which were nonfiction), only 2 entered her language arts classroom (both fiction).

Lauren and Tiffany gained status because they refused to perform in the ways that school had envisioned as appropriate behaviors. Angie and Carrie gained status because they did choose to perform in socially sanctioned ways. Their written work and projects clearly revealed more time and thought; yet, in order to coopt the school authorities, they shared their homework, allowing it to be copied by Tiffany and the others. Carrie liked to write and owned a computer, so she wrote and sold stories for the others to hand in. In this way, each queen could sustain her role by defying the authoritative presence.

Because of their unfaltering allegiance to their friends, they would not break out of the roles and expectations as established by the group. Also, just as they used literacy to establish themselves as separate from adults, it was equally important for these girls to separate themselves from other groups perceived as less adolescent, and often this was ac-complished through literacy.

SUMMARY AND CONCLUSION

Ask them if they read and they will say no. They'll tell you they don't like to write, but volumes of notes they have written to each other remain cherished, stuffed in shoeboxes under their beds. None of this was what they were supposed to be doing in school, and the passion they exhibited for these tasks was never evident in the sanctioned liter-ate tasks.

Hurrying to be seen as young women rather than as little girls, the social queens used literacy to gain power in this arena. Literacy served to document an official passage into adolescence. Out-of-bounds from adults, literacy intertwined with out-of-bounds desires. Bathed as these girls were in a set of societal norms for women, it should be hardly surprising that romance and sexuality were key themes in note-passing, graffiti writing, and zine reading. Throughout their literate underlife, Tiffany, Angie, and Lauren wrote what they would not pronounce. Their writing created a physical distance that separated them from their text and allowed them to reflect on a language that they considered powerful and adult.

On the top of one note, for example, written boldly in red ink, was this message, "This note requires parental guidance to read, so ask you're (*sic*) mom First!" Then in the body of the note, which was written in green ink, was the word "fuck" written three times in red ink. The writer very consciously changed pens each time she made a deliberate decision to write the word.

The queens were aware of their control over their language. Through literacy, they played with power. Much of this writing conveyed a strong sense of play in constructing messages on paper or on the wall, which stood in sharp contrast to the authoritative discourse of the institution. Such play with language most often focused on body images and body functions, things that are most out of the control of early adolescents. They wrote in resistance to authoritative discourse as they wrote their way into adulthood. Like the Smithton women reading romances (Radway, 1984), the social queens used literacy as a "declaration of their independence." Literacy served them as a powerful tool to gain status and group solidarity. In review, the common themes in literacy events are: (1) Literacy is a social event with same-age peers; (2) literacy is used to mark special status; and (3) literacy is used to sustain social roles.

First, as a social event, exhibitions of literacy were often constructed together in the presence of their intended audience, an intimate group of like-minded peers. Social queens rarely—and never by choice—engaged in solitary activities, literate or otherwise. Individual assignments were often written together in the lunch room, on the bus, over the telephone. Copying homework and "borrowing" and "giving away" stories were common practices. At times borrowing was seen as an act of resistance; at other times, it was simply an act of friendship. Nevertheless, the exchange of papers was most often perceived as a matter of saving time, with little regard for any opportunity to learn from each other. Group projects and group work were highly prized by the queens, who valued the time spent together in class and the legitimate excuse to get together after school. If any entertained a desire for solitude, such feelings remained masked.

Second, as a marker of status, literacy was counted: Who wrote the most; who received the most; who owned the most, first. Just as notes were counted to assess popularity, low quiz scores were praised as markers of defiance; yet, the queens valued their social time together for sports, dances, and other social events, and thus had to calculate the risks to remain mobile by acquiring the grades necessary to avoid trouble at home. Midterm notices, forms sent home by teachers to inform parents or caregivers that grades were low, were a highly regarded symbol of status because they documented a lack of concern for academics. While such forms curtailed their out-of-school activities and thus had to be reckoned with cautiously, they documented an act of defiance, an act in direct opposition to institutional sanctions.

Third, social roles were defined in terms of group solidarity, measured by those left outside as much as those called into the inner circle. For example, the queens (with the exception of Lauren, who rarely carried a reading book to language arts class) carried R. L. Stine books to class because it had been established that they "are cool" while other books such as Lauren's sports books remained hidden.

For the social queens, literate underlife carried much more currency, more access to power, than any school-sanctioned literacy. School-sanctioned literacy was coopted and reduced in order for the queens to maintain the structure of their social world. Both sanctioned literacy and literate underlife utilized tools to create and maintain social roles. For the queens there were two kinds of texts: "[the] kind you hafta do and [the] kind you wanna do." This division represented a distinction between texts that were assigned by teachers and texts "assigned" by the group. Both kinds of texts were clearly perceived as social. Selection of either carried social expectations and obligations and consequences.

The social role embraced by the queens constricted literate practices and intellectual engagement. The following conversation echoes the tensions that complicate literacy instruction for the social queens:

M.F.: What are you reading in language arts now?

ANGIE: I just grab something from Tiffany's locker cause I haven't started any. I haven't read anything for about two weeks. I just carried something around for about two weeks.

M.F.: What book is it? What are you carrying now?

ANGIE: Umm? I don't know. I just grab one. Probably R. L. Stine. That's what Tiffany usually has.

M.F. [To Lauren]: Do you have a book that you are taking to your language arts class?

LAUREN: Ummm no. He [Mr. Staton] has a cart of books.

M.F.: Are you reading anything in there?

LAUREN: NO! I DON'T READ!

M.F.: What do you do when he says you have reading time?

LAUREN: Write.

M.F.: What kinds of stuff are you writing?

LAUREN: Notes.

M.F.: Is that all right with Mr. Staton if you write notes in there?

LAUREN [laughs]: No, he thinks I am writing stories.

In summary, because the queens privileged group identity over individual identity, allegiance to peer groups was central, as illustrated by the comment "what Tiffany usually has." Likewise, when Lauren boldly announced, "No! I don't read!" she was announcing her role as a resisting student. From the perspective of the queens, only two social roles were available within the school context: little kids (those who follow the rules) and teenagers (those who make and break the rules). By virtue of their entry into junior high, queens regarded themselves as teenagers who must coopt sanctioned literacy, always seeking ways to make it a part of the literate underlife, in opposition to the official rules and regulations of the institution.

Since the queens' reason for being was located primarily in the social realm, literacy was used to connect them to their peers. Print, for the queens, granted authority to the word and thus became a useful tool to document and maintain social roles—fixing relationships in print if only temporarily, as friendships and romances slid and slipped within this peer network. Social relationships were the central focus for the queens and in a school context that constrained face-to-face interactions, literacy functioned to maintain such tight connectedness to peers and also to deny any such connections to adults.

CHAPTER 4

Literacy and the Tough Cookies

A keen sense of pride in individual accomplishments and a refusal to accept assistance or acknowledge outside influence marked the discourse of the tough cookies. Self-reliance permeated their conversations and worked against any sense of social connectedness. Throughout the year, I often puzzled over their sense of friendship.

"Take care of yourself" was a strong theme that ran throughout Cleo and Dottie's lives. The belief that few will assist made it imperative to instill a value in self-determination. Cleo's mother put it this way:

> She's gotta do it herself. It's her education, not mine. I've had to teach her to take care of herself. . . . She's almost an adult and I get the impression that they [the teachers] want me to walk her through her work. And it's not that I don't care either. I really do. I think it's important, but I don't think it's my place.

Throughout the year, Cleo's mother emphasized Cleo's independence. From the cookies' perspective, one considered herself to be at her best when she was taking care of herself, most likely alone or in the presence of adults. Mrs. Zmoleck observed this sense of denial of peer influence in Cleo:

> Maybe I've been watching her more closely now because of you. But I've noticed this week that she has worn the same pair of pants with big holes in them, and it just seems like she doesn't have to do that. Like she wants to be outside the group. That she wants to appear different from the other girls.

THE LIFEWORLD OF THE TOUGH COOKIES

Debunking the popular belief that adolescents seek close connections with same-age peers, Cleo operated from a set of assumptions that insisted she deny peer influence and connections. Similarly, Dottie's actions denied the commonly held assumption that adolescents sever ties with adults. Dottie's mother described her perceptions of Dottie in the following manner:

> She sees school as a very important thing. I think that she wants to excel and do good, and she wants to make her teachers proud of her, and she wants to understand and do a good job. That's the main thing.

This quote reveals two key themes that emerged repeatedly in conversations with the cookies: a focus on academics and striving for adult approval. Throughout this study, a strong sense of connectedness to significant adults emerged again and again. As Cleo and Dottie entered junior high, their primary allegiance remained with their mothers, who were explicitly training them to rely on themselves, to operate primarily within the family network, and to remove themselves from the influence of peer groups.

Along with the strong message to take care of yourself came a seemingly inconsistent message: a reliance on family and the necessity of sticking together. Peer groups served a function at school, but the cookies did not perceive them to be an integral part of their daily routines. In response to the question about friendships, ''Do you think a person can ever be as close to a friend as she is to her family?'' in separate interviews, Cleo and Dottie confirmed this emerging assumption:

DOTTIE: Well, maybe. See, they might be like closer to their mother than to their friends. I don't know. 'Cause I'm more closer to my mom than to my friends.
CLEO: It depends on how their family is to them. Because if they have a rotten family, they probably can be very close to their friends.

Notice that, for Cleo, a close friendship with someone outside the family was possible only when a qualifier existed such as ''they have a rotten family.'' The social aspects of school life were viewed very differently by the cookies than by the queens. For the cookies, relationships with significant adults were more important than with same-age peers. Unlike the queens, the cookies' reason for being at school was located primarily in the academic realm. Close connections with teachers were considered important ties for academic success.

Acknowledging the change from sixth to seventh grade, the cookies expressed a sense of loss for the close ties they had felt with Mr. Stone, their sixth-grade teacher. The cookies regularly expressed their strong belief that getting a good education will lead to increased chances for a college education and thus a more secure future. The notion that improving skills would improve the future was generally expressed as a solitary quest, expressed in the singular, always carrying the sense of going it alone. Dottie, for example, said, "My mom says there won't be money for college. So I'm gonna get a job next year. You can sack groceries when you turn 14."

For the tough cookies, individual identity was privileged over group membership: "I did this all by myself," "If anybody gives me an idea, I reject it. It has to be my own." Such comments reveal the tremendous sense of pressure they felt to perform unassisted. This created a sense of pride among the cookies, who resisted collaboration and denied influence. In interviews, the cookies preferred to be interviewed alone as the following quote reveals:

CLEO: You're gonna just talk to me and not Dottie?
M.F.: Yes. I'd like to talk to each of you alone.
CLEO: Yeah, cause you can't be yourself exactly.

Again and again, the cookies refuted one of the most commonly held assumptions about adolescents—the growing significance of same-age peers.

By virtue of the cookies' residence in trailer parks, teachers often believed they had been cast from the same mold. The assumption that these girls shared a common culture was, of course, reinforced by their self-selected friends. "You ever notice that trailer-park girls are all friends?" one teacher commented to me. The categorization "trailer-park girls" carried with it the implicit assumptions of a shared common culture. This perception was in part true. Dottie and Cleo did consistently claim each other as best friend, and indeed they shared many beliefs. Yet, it might be suggested that the tough cookies were recognized as a social group within the school context not simply because of the shared values for family life and independence, but because opportunities to join other groups were denied them within the institutional structure. Unable to participate in social events due to economic constraints, home obligations, and lack of available transportation, it seems that the cookies were friends at least partly because they could not choose to join other groups.

Allegiance to families both connected and divided the cookies. For the most part, these girls' best friends were not available in the junior high school setting. In their daily routines they most often turned to their mothers and sisters. Perhaps gender-role distinctions further re-moved the cookies from the social networks available within the school context, since differences between gender roles may be more marked in working-class homes (Schlegel & Barry, 1991).

Distinct gender roles were clearly visible and openly articulated in these homes where women maintain the household and raise the chil-dren. Throughout this year-long study, Dottie and Cleo both expressed and enacted their ties to their homes, especially to their mothers. Nei-ther Dottie's stepfather nor Cleo's father attended school conferences. They were not at home when I visited and did not choose to actively participate. Cleo's mother described the situation this way: "He's [Cleo's father] not very good with them [the children]. I don't think he wanted kids. So Cleo was the one that always took care of everybody else." Similarly, Dottie's mother described her husband as inactive in the family. While both teens and mothers talked about the importance of family, the construction of family focused on the female members.

Dottie's identity was greatly shaped by her interactions with her mother, younger sister, and grandmother. She spent her leisure time at home, and she regularly remarked that she was looking forward to spending a weekend at her grandmother's house. Parties to which I was invited were exclusively for women and girls. Clearly, Dottie's home was the woman's domain and children were women's business.

Cleo and her mother shared a strong commitment to feminist issues. As the primary wage-earner and caretaker, Cleo's mother often ex-pressed concern for her daughter's success in a "male world," concern for how little things had changed since she was a teen. She continued to harbor resentment because her father paid for a college education for her brothers but not for her; as she described it, "I was supposed to just get married and have babies." Her anger emerged in conversations in which both she and Cleo openly acknowledged concern that Art, Cleo's eight-year-old brother, was growing up to be a "chauvinist pig."

For the cookies, leisure activities and work responsibilities centered on their family ties, leaving little time and few activities in common with school peers. As best friends, Dottie and Cleo shared few social activi-ties. During the full year in which I observed them, they spent out-of-school time together only when I arranged it and on the occasion that each celebrated her birthday. The half-mile distance on a busy four-lane highway that separated their homes prohibited walking or biking. Be-cause of the schedule of the school day, they shared only 20 minutes together every other day during their lunch time.

As sixth graders, Dottie and Cleo had played together at recess and sat beside each other in the classroom. The structure of the school day in junior high worked against sustaining peer networks for the cookies, who were able to socialize only at school. Mothers and daughters were keenly aware of this change in school structure that constricted friendships. Kara, Dottie's mother, observed:

> Her and Cleo and Beth and Pat, they used to do things together, but not at all this year. I noticed that. I think a lot of that's the change at junior high. Cause in elementary school they have recess and a lot of things together, and now they don't.

Since there was no longer any recess time, it was difficult for them to maintain friendships. Dottie described what was for her one of the biggest changes in the move to junior high:

> Well, I think that my friends this year. I've lost some friends, and it's just a sudden change. Um, like Cleo, I think she might still be my friend. I don't know. It's just that we haven't been talking. We don't have any classes together. And that's about it. I don't see her.

The cookies' school world was sharply demarcated from their home world. Cleo's mother articulated the division between home and school in the following way:

> School's only a part. It's like going to work, you know. You're only there so much, but the whole idea is to go to work *for* your family. I think that's the most important part. That's what we go through life for. . . . It seems like this society and schools and employers work and they try to take it all away from you, and I don't understand that. I mean they are my kids first, and I will do what I have to for their good. . . . I always hear them talking about, "Well, we have to mold them this way and mold them that way." And I refuse to let them.

Here, tensions are apparent. The family's position was in opposition to the school, in an us/them dichotomy. School was viewed as the villain in this story attempting to "mold" her daughter away from her. Yet, Cleo's mother clearly acknowledged the value of education "for the family." Her refusal to "let them" implies a firm border between the home and the school worlds.

For the cookies, this boundary remained firmly in place for two reasons: First, outside school, work and play were set within multiage groups where hierarchies were explicitly acknowledged and understood (see similar finding for working-class students in the work of Eckert, 1989) and second, a strong sense of autonomy existed in these homes, where as young children they had been expected to make decisions about cooking, cleaning, and caring for siblings.

The discourse of adolescence claims a greater need for autonomy with the arrival of adolescence, yet the cookies have been gaining autonomy since a much younger age, as illustrated by this statement by Cleo's mother: "I've never really had trouble with Cleo 'cause she grew up fast. I mean she's been pretty much taking care of herself since she went to kindergarten."

Hence, roles available in the home were viewed very differently from those at school. The guiding social structures in the home were denied in the context of the school. For these reasons, movements between the two contexts created tensions for the cookies, who felt most confident and comfortable at home. Because expectations were perceived as very different in the two contexts, the cookies were keenly aware of competing roles and regularly expressed their discomfort with the "person" they have to be at school. Dottie said, "Well, at school I'm not myself. But at home, I'm more open to myself than at school. I'm just a whole different person." Dottie explained that at home she could be less guarded, more comfortable, and, as she said on multiple occasions, "just more myself."

The sharp contrast between home and school was evident in the incongruent portraits of these girls in the two contexts. This social group was perceived very differently from the point of view of teachers—who consistently described them as "nice girls"—than from the point of view of their mothers—who regularly acknowledged their independence. It seems almost impossible to imagine that tough cookies and nice girls could describe the same individuals. One carries implications of a grit, a steadfastness, a stubbornness if you will, while the other implies docility. Because of the ways that the cookies staged their performances at school, teachers might not recognize their mothers' descriptions of them. Dottie's language arts teacher described her in the following way:

> She's a mouse. She's a sweetie. I mean she's not afraid to talk. She'll talk in small groups. She'll talk to me, but she's just a little mouse.

Her mother, on the other hand, recognizing the multiple "sides of her," described her this way:

> One side of her, the school side is very quiet. This side of her at home is very loud. I think if she's in an atmosphere where she

knows people, she is more assertive and talkative. When she doesn't know somebody, she won't say anything. But she's very outgoing. She can raise Holy Cain!

The phrase "where she knows people" makes visible tensions created by the fact that the structure of the junior high school does not allow the close connections between teacher and students that would make Dottie feel most comfortable.

Like Dottie, Cleo acknowledged a tremendous gap between the "side" that she presented at school and the "side" she displayed at home. In the following poem, Cleo struggled with her perceptions of who she was supposed to be at school:

> Sides
> Allow me to introduce Impeccable Intellect
> She is flawless
> Ideal
> A model student
> I am her mirror
> She is my shield
> My mask
> For I am not faultless
> She abandons me each day
> She journeys where people hide
> Behind their masks
> Called
> Me

Cleo's use of such words as "shield," "mask," and "mirror" illustrates how she constructed her school role, concealing herself within the school context. This "side" of herself, as she described it, was completely in control, completely taking care of herself, "impeccable" and "flawless." Because she considered the impressions that she made on teachers to be central to her school role, vulnerability was reserved for more secure contexts. At school she felt that she must present herself as flawless. Cleo interpreted this poem—written at home and not shared with Mrs. Zmoleck, her language arts teacher—in this way:

It's almost like there are multiple people, like there are multiple me's, and this is the one that goes to school, and this is what other people expect.

An overt awareness of herself as hiding her vulnerabilities at school is evident in Cleo's poem and in her interpretation. She not only acknowledged shifting selves in different contexts, but she was aware that she had been cast into a school role by others: "This is what other people expect," she said of her school self.

LITERATE PRACTICES

The strong themes that shaped the cookies' social roles and relationships spilled over onto their assumptions about literacy. The message to "take care of yourself" influenced all aspects of school and home life. Common themes with regard to literacy learning were guided by a recurrent message: (1) construction of a text is a solitary and private affair; (2) literacy denies allegiance and influence; (3) literacy is guarded to protect from self-disclosure.

Beyond the school setting, the tough cookies used literacies for playing, escaping from domestic chores, and capturing experiences in print. Within the school setting, the cookies used literacy in a traditional sense that matched the school's construction of literacy learning, using literacy to acquire information, display competence, and discover meaning. The cookies envisioned for themselves a specific, concrete plan for success. On numerous occasions, I heard comments such as this one: "If you get good grades, you can get a college scholarship." They read and wrote to succeed in school, which would lead, they believed, to success in the larger culture. All of this was built on their unfaltering faith in the opportunity structure of schooling.

The stereotyped image that dominates popular beliefs about low-income families, characterizing them as nonliterate, could not be found in the trailers I visited. The homes that I visited were print-rich. Cleo's trailer, like a tiny, crowded library filled with novels, textbooks, dictionaries, anthologies, poetry, and magazines, overflowed into a shed in their backyard built especially to house books. One had to look a bit harder to find the print-rich sources in Dottie's tidy trailer. Stacks of magazines that served as integral elements of her family's social world were always neatly hidden away in closets and dresser drawers.

While sharing many underlying beliefs about life and literacy, the cookies' families should not be viewed as a unified community. Clearly they shared many values, but how those values were enacted in the daily routines of the family were quite distinct. With literacy as the lens, individual portraits of the cookies emerged. As difficult as it is to present any individualized portraits of the social queens, it is equally difficult to group the literate practices of the cookies together.

LITERACIES BEYOND THE SANCTIONS

Those literate practices of the cookies that were not immediately recognized as school literacy should not be described as out of bounds. While the cookies wrote beyond the sanctions, they did not write overtly in resistance to or in opposition to the school-sanctioned practices. The cookies fully embraced the school-sanctioned role of good student, a role they believed would assure them present success and lead later to success in college and beyond. When asked about following rules, Cleo and Dottie admitted breaking rules at home but not at school. Cleo denied ever breaking a rule at school. Shame-faced, Dottie, on the other hand, admitted that she had chewed gum once. So in the school context, they did not work against the institutional model. They embraced it, aligning themselves with teachers, often in opposition to peers.

The following list, lifted from interview and classroom transcripts, reveals the roles available for girls in the school context, from the perspective of the cookies:

popular blonde girls   real girls
beach buddies   good students
popular air heads
bubble-headed girls
richy-rich
snobs

The labels on the left were all different names for the same role—that of a girl who pursues friendships at the expense of academic pursuits. Notice that, from the perspective of the cookies, the designation "popular" for those who engage with same-age peers connotes a lack of academic interest. The role of good student, on the other hand, was equivalent to that of "real girl." Real and popular were mutually exclusive terms. This meant, of course, that to be a popular girl, one could not be herself. Popularity was perceived as artificial. Obviously, the cookies saw themselves as real girls. Real girls worked hard in school to achieve their academic goals, unencumbered by the constraints that accompanied popularity, uninfluenced by other girls.

Literate practices were perceived as avenues to academic success; yet, beyond the sanctions, home literacy practices were constructed very differently from the school practices, and unknowingly, at times, worked against sanctioned practices.

Dottie's Home Literacies

Magazines filled with photographs of country homes and portraits of beautiful interiors of living rooms, kitchens, and bedrooms, along with catalogs from Home Interiors, Inc., were the primary reading materials of Dottie and her mother, Kara. Kara explained her reading habits this way, "I read books, but I don't read book-books. I read books and magazines about cooking and I like to read about country homes."

She explained the distinction between books and book-books. Books were what she read—magazines and information to beautify her home. This reading consisted of cookbooks, home decorating guides, and magazines. "Book-books" designated those things she did not read. They were, in her words, "what you are supposed to read. You know, what they made you read in school. What you have to read in school. I wasn't very good at it. You know, *long* novels." Notice how Kara constructed reading. Novels were ranked more highly than any necessary reading to transact business. Novels for her continued to be "what you are supposed to read." Still carrying her school-based training and her self-assessment as "not very good at it," Kara sharply distinguished between reading fiction (the only thing that counts as reading book-books) and her own reading, judging her own practices as less valued.

According to Kara's definition of literacy, she did not read much. Although she spent many hours reading magazines and cookbooks, she did not count most of her reading as reading. She would not include her Home Interiors parties in any discussion of literacy events. Neither would she count the reading and writing necessary to manage social service forms and legal documents, or the leisure hours that she spent with her daughters leafing through the Home Interiors catalogues.

Because Home Interiors, Inc., depended on print sources for their parties, sales, and promotions, I include their events in my definition of literacy while acknowledging that neither Kara nor Dottie would include them. The activities surrounding the planning and hosting of such events filled much of the time that Dottie and her mother spent together. Such parties were, in fact, one of the most frequent literacy events in Dottie's home. They were a primary source of entertainment for Dottie and the women in her extended family and neighborhood. Pages of the spiral notebook on the kitchen counter displayed elaborate "wall groupings": wall arrangements of mirrors, pictures, shelves, twining vines, votive cups, candle holders, and figurines.

My first invitation to Dottie's home was to attend a Home Interiors party. I parked in front of their double-wide trailer and walked up the steps. Inside, their trailer matched many of the wall groupings printed on my invitation brochure, a 16-page full-color booklet with illustrated wall groupings, listing hundreds of bathroom, kitchen, living room, and bedroom items for sale. Like the other rooms in the home, the walls in Dottie's room reflected the care and time that she spent with her mother planning their Home Interior purchases and designing their wall space to display them attractively. Dottie's home was filled with brass candle holders, wooden shelves, ceramic birds and bears, mauve flowers, greenery, framed prints, and small mirrors.

A sense of the home as an exclusively women's domain emerged in conversations surrounding this event in Dottie's home. This was apparent in the Home Interiors literature as well. "There is a place for you," one booklet suggested. Beneath a red rose, the booklet goes on as follows:

Our Code of Ethics
We believe in the dignity and importance of women . . .
We believe that everything woman touches should be ennobled by that touch . . .
We believe that the home is the greatest influence on the character of mankind . . .
We believe that the home should be a haven—a place of refuge, a place of peace, a place of harmony, a place of beauty . . .
No home in America ever need be dull and unattractive.
We are dedicated to doing our part to make every home have ATTRACTION POWER!

MARY C. CROWLEY

Dottie's mother, Kara, was a homemaker who took a great deal of pride in keeping her home comfortable and attractive. She embraced the role for women that Mary C. Crowley had envisioned for her. In order to afford to decorate her home in the manner she desired, Kara hosted home decorating parties. As the Home Interiors literature suggests:

There's a world of free gifts awaiting you as a Home Interiors hostess. Just share your home for a few hours during the day or evening so your personal Displayer can present our decorative accessories to you and your friends.

You earn valuable Merits by having a Home Interiors Show. Merits are earned based on the level of sales and the number of future Show Bookings. Merits can be used just like cash to receive Hostess Gifts.

More than simply earning merits to be used "just like cash," Dottie and her mother looked forward to social aspects of hosting parties. On several occasions, Dottie, her sister, her mother, her aunt, her grandmother, her cousin, her neighbor, her neighbor's daughter, my two daughters, and I came together in the living room of Kara's trailer for just such an event.

On Sunday afternoons in Hillside Estates, groups of women gathered to share each other's company and pass on a set of rituals and rules to their daughters. Each party began with a reading of a poem by the displayer employed by the company—known by all as "the Home Interiors Lady"—who then presented a red rose to the hostess. The Home Interiors Lady then announced, "We'll go around the room, introduce ourselves and say what wall we are thinking of." Each person in the room, in turn, introduced herself, announced her relationship to Kara, and named one wall: "I'm Cindy, Kara's aunt, and I'm thinking of my bathroom." The next woman announced, "I'm Kara's neighbor, Carol Lynn, and I want to work on my living room wall." Later, I understood that the opening ritual of naming one wall was based on economic necessity. Most women came to buy one item for one particular wall because these items were not inexpensive.

After introductions had been made, Nancy, the Home Interiors Lady, handed out larger versions of the invitation booklets, announcing "our newest accessories," as she gave to each person $50 worth of "funny money" printed on brightly colored paper. She would then select one of the new items for sale, challenging the women with something like: "Now, the first one who can tell me what page this Banbury Mirrored Sconce is on"—pointing to a brass, mirrored candle holder that she hooked to the portable wall brought with her to practice making wall groupings—"I will give you ten more dollars." She waved gold paper cut slightly smaller than legal tender. All immediately began turning the pages of the booklet. Kara's aunt was most often first, because, as Kara explained, she has so many parties she knew where everything was.

Funny money was used to participate in an auction for a door prize at the end of the evening. A subtle hint of competition among extended family members emerged when the women began commenting about how many items they already had. As the distribution of funny money continued, competition was less subtle. In fact, on one occasion, Dottie and her sister Jackie fought over who had earned the most funny money and who was then entitled to "buy" the door prize. Because the goal was to earn the greatest amount of funny money by the end of the evening, talk was kept to a minimum and collaboration was nonexistent.

First, the Home Interiors Lady made wall groupings on a three-foot by three-foot display wall. In the center of the living room, she hooked a framed print onto the wall and began accessorizing it by adding a small shelf below, candles or mirrors on either side, a swag above or below with figurines, artificial flowers, and wooden book accents on the shelf. While this event was social, it was not collaborative. As with the earlier competition, in order to be the first to shout out answers to Nancy's questions, talk was constricted. As the Home Interiors Lady grouped items on her portable wall, she asked, "Now, how many different colors of wood can you have on one wall at a time? I will give $20 if you can tell me."

All of the women and girls, except for my daughters and me, raised their hands. Nancy called on Jackie. "Seven," she said. Nancy confirmed that she was right, repeating, "Seven—you can have seven different colors of wood on one wall." Then as she placed a second small shelf next to the first one, she asked, "How far apart can you hang things on your wall?" Again hands went up. "A palm's length" was the correct answer because, as Nancy explained,

> you want to be able to read your wall, and you don't want to read [pausing between each word] "The cat ate the mouse." You want to read [no longer pausing] "The cat ate the mouse," and so your items must be close together so your eyes can read the wall.

Using the metaphor of reading, Nancy worked to convince these women that for fluency they needed to buy many items to make their walls easily read—items to be segmented by a mere palm's length.

As the party progressed, the Home Interiors Lady called on women by first name to assist her—"Julie, which do you like better, the Hearts of Love Sconces or the Tassel Mirrored Sconces?" "Dottie, do you want to work with 'Let Us Go In Love?' [a framed print with roses, butterflies, and a poem]." As she asked for opinions, she continued to turn attention back to the sales book with the frequent opportunity to earn more funny money.

Nancy invited guests to take turns decorating the wall. When a young girl such as Dottie or her sister was invited to "decorate it the way you want it," she was often corrected by a woman because "the shelf is too low" or the "candle comes up too high on the picture." After all guests had as many opportunities as they wanted to create wall groupings, they counted up their funny money, and the door prize was auctioned to the highest bidder. The party concluded with coffee, punch, and individuals' purchasing items. Conversation centered on what was going to be purchased and who would host the next party.

An examination of this literacy event reveals several elements beneath the party atmosphere that impact on Dottie's identity and on her ideas about social interactions around literacy. First, most of the talk was competitive, right-answer talk. Opinions did not allow for individual expression. Nancy initiated the sequence by calling on a guest to assist her. The guest then responded with a short, most often one-word answer, and finally Nancy evaluated the correctness of the answer. Conversations at the party resemble Mehan's IRE (Initiate, Respond, Evaluate) pattern of lesson structure in which the teacher initiates discussion, the student responds, and then the teacher evaluates the student's response (see Cazden, 1988, pp. 29–36). While Mehan argues that this pattern is part of classroom talk and is not found in informal conversation, the IRE pattern predominated in these party conversations. Talk at these events generally consisted of oral fill-in-the-blanks. Such a match between informal talk and school talk directly impacted the way Dottie perceived her role in conversations around a text at school. From Dottie's perspective, texts are received as authority, and, as Bakhtin (1981) argues, such an authoritative function of discourse is always a matter of the reader's perspective; yet, any sense of wrestling and wrangling with texts was absent.

Second, the Home Interiors Lady's words were received as authority, and women deferred to her. She transmitted her knowledge about the latest decorating secrets, stating, for example, quite matter-of-factly, "Mauve is the color of the nineties." Such interactions focused on Nancy, the Home Interiors representative, who occupied center stage. Talk was planned and controlled by the displayer, who held higher status than the others. No one ever disagreed with her publicly. No one asked how she knew such information. No one ever said, "Why is seven the correct number of colors of wood on one wall?" In public, the women and girls may have said that they preferred one wall grouping over another, but they never suggested that they did not agree with Nancy's conception of beauty.

Through this literacy event, we see a role designed for women. As the Home Interiors literature suggested, there is "a place for you" through "attraction power." In a community of like-minded women, literacy was used to regulate desire. Literacy offered the opportunity of controlling one's social position. Gender behaviors were socially ordered and policed through the pages of Home Interiors advertisements.

Received from an outside authority, literacy was a commodity that held the promise of achieving confidence through, as the Home Interiors literature suggests, "purchasing power."

Backstage, in a corner of the kitchen, Dottie on occasion smiled and whispered, "I didn't like that Christmas swag, did you?" Her mother also whispered similar comments. Yet, on a public stage, all women deferred to Nancy's authority. I did not observe any women or girls challenge Nancy's authority, question her ideas, or disagree with her opinions. This event brought women together to share a public sense of shared community. Yet, dissent did emerge backstage. In the presence of authority, deference was the norm. Such training for women, it seems, is part of the larger culture in which women allocate dissent to backstage regions.

Beneath the social aspects of this literacy event in Dottie's household rested the socioeconomic issues. Status was built into the event with a predominance of talk about the price of each item and attention was given to the items that were perceived to match those in the homes of the wealthy. From this one event, we see how women's roles in Dottie's household were constructed through purchasing commodities.

Because of limited economic resources, these women were seizing control over the one domain in which they did hold power—their living rooms. By controlling the wall space in their homes, they were importing the socioeconomic status of affluence. Display of wealth emerged in the talk that surrounded the parties. Women talked about the "gilded prints that you might pay over $300 for" that they could purchase for just $25.95.

The sense of affluence through home decorating spilled over onto economic constructions of literacy. Most women had purchased a set of wooden books, three for $8.95, because, as Nancy explained, "See how the gold draws out the rich colors of your wall." These books did not open and, as Nancy reported, could serve two purposes: (1) to draw out the colors of other items and (2) to set things on, elevating figurines to make the wall match the standards for attraction power. Using literacy for decorative purposes is not unlike what many others do in displaying expensive coffee-table books or rare first editions. Yet the richness of the wooden books is contrasted with the urgent need for economic security in a home in which, temporarily, neither parent earned income. Issues of economics shaped the interactions—choosing one wall, buying gold items, earning funny money. Because so much was beyond the economic means of these women, the rhetoric of Home Interiors fed a need for display of autonomy, control, and affluence.

Gathered in the living room with family and neighbors, engaged in searching texts for right answers and correct page numbers, Dottie must have sensed a parallel with school literacy. Opinions were not, in fact, opinions at all. They were right answers remembered from previous encounters with the materials. Texts and adults held authority. The authority figure in the room held superior knowledge and control of the opinions of all others. Repeated experiences in which one was told that her idea was not the correct opinion matched the practice that Dottie used in school, a practice for which she was labeled quiet and less confident. For Dottie, the perceived way to succeed was to keep quiet until you were sure of the right answer.

The public nature of this event was training for Dottie in both literacy and life. Central to the construction of identity was a home and family identity. Yet, like the working-class girls in Weiss's (1993) study, in which "the girls' identity . . . exhibits a beginning challenge to the domestic code—that code under which home or family is defined as women's place and the public sphere of power and work as men's place" (p. 103), Dottie regularly articulated her desire for economic gain.

Finally, examination of this literacy event reveals that social events are not necessarily constructed as collaborative. Competition prevented a sense of cooperation or sharing. Dottie carried this model of social interaction with her into the classroom. When she was expected to interact in groups she exhibited: (1) a deference to received authority and (2) construction of all social events as a stage for individual performances. For Dottie, reading and writing remained a private affair.

In addition to Home Interiors parties, Dottie's primary literate practice was writing poetry. Literacy served two key functions for Dottie: to escape her immediate surroundings and to discover her feelings. She wrote poetry because, as she explained, "I get so mad. I just go in my room, slam the door and write and write until I'm not mad anymore." Whispers of the Home Interiors parties echoed as Dottie explained that writing poetry was for her an escape from the world in which she lived. "I just write until I don't think about things anymore," she explained.

Most often the act of constructing a text served its purpose and then she just "ripped it up and threw it away." Once a poem was written, her purposes had been met. She rarely saved what she wrote at home. From Dottie's home experiences, we see the following key features: (1) Public literacy is competitive—it serves to document right-answer thinking; (2) private literacy is self-disclosure and should be protected from the view of others.

Cleo's Home Literacies

Cleo's single-wide trailer was crammed with books and magazines and pamphlets and stray papers. Judy, her mother, built the storage shed behind their home to store the surplus books that wouldn't fit into their home. Judy exchanged paperback novels with her coworkers at the cereal factory where she worked. With her mother, younger brother, and sister, Cleo visited the library almost weekly. Money was budgeted for school-book orders, and books ranked high on each family member's holiday gift list. "I can always come up with money for that," explained Judy.

Judy regarded books as tools to instill positive values in her children: "Not just for school, not just for learning but for pleasure and to help them lead a better life." Judy defined a better life as a more humane understanding of people who had been oppressed and marginalized. Books, according to Judy, "help you get beyond yourself. And if you can get beyond yourself, you can handle it." She viewed books as a way to expand her world and that of her children. Cleo's mother used books to help her children learn about their Jewish heritage. Likewise, she wanted her daughters to understand the plight of women and she regularly turned their attention to books about the women's movement. Books by and about Native Americans, African-Americans, Jews, and women lined the bookshelf beside the sofa. Judy explained:

> I spent three years in the service, and I saw prejudice and stuff there, and it never ends, it never stops. . . . I mean I just heard something last night at work about Jews, you know. And I won't tolerate it.

It was difficult to navigate around their living room where books crowded the sofa, cluttered the floor, and teetered atop the desk. All members of Cleo's family were both avid pleasure readers and avid information readers. Cleo and her mother usually had two or three books-in-progress. Judy described her reading habits:

> One time I had six of them going. Get bored with one, put it down and pick up one of the other ones. I remember my mom doing that, too. She had books stuffed everywhere.

Cleo explained that each reading fulfilled particular emotional needs: "It depends upon my mood, like if I'm happy, I'll want to read something like *Anne of Green Gables*. Not something like *Small Sacrifices*."

Her mother read paperback novels to relax and often had a history text in progress to, as she said, "expand horizons." Judy regularly talked about "stretching" her children through books. The values she placed on reading are illustrated in the following quote:

> I don't care if they [her children] ever use it. I mean, I think it's great to learn. I think it expands your horizons so you're not stuck in the narrowness. I mean that's the biggest thing. I don't want them to be narrow. I don't want them to be prisoners.

Her choice of the metaphor "prisoners" reveals her strong attitude about books as freeing agents.

Cleo described her reading this way:

> Sometimes I just pick up a book and read it. I don't really care what the type is. Like if I don't have anything to read, I just go roaming around the house looking for something good. I know it frustrates my mom, but I just read anything.

Clearly aware of her mother's attitude about books as liberating, Cleo acknowledged her own lighter reading practices. Judy noted the value of this kind of reading too:

> I try to stretch her, but sometimes she just wants to read something to escape, to make herself feel better. I still let her read them. I don't tell her that she can't. But I tell her she does have to read other stuff.

Cleo also regularly turned to magazines for information about cats, sewing, cooking, and computers, yet she insisted that she didn't read them. "I don't really read them. I look at them. I think of reading as, you know, reading." She held a definition that "reading as reading" meant reading cover-to-cover.

While she denied that scanning a magazine for information was reading, she also denied reading what someone had suggested. The following transcript illustrates Cleo's commitment to her tough-cookie script that regards input from others as a sign of weakness:

M.F.: Anybody suggest good books for you?
CLEO: My mom suggests books a lot, but I don't read the books she wants.
M.F.: Is that a change from last year? Did you share more last year?
CLEO: No.

While reading was most often constructed as a solo endeavor, on occasion Cleo spent time reading to her younger brother, who was just becoming an independent reader. She also regularly visited Sharon, her next-door neighbor who, due to cerebral palsy, was most often bedridden. Cleo read to Sharon, although she acknowledged that "we don't read that long because she gets tired. I think she likes me there, but I don't think it matters what I read." Back at home, Cleo returned again and again to one of her favorite books, *Karen*, an adolescent novel about a girl with cerebral palsy. Clearly personal ties were drawn through reading.

Books were the cornerstone of this home. Through them, each member found escape, knowledge, connection, and the ability to grow. "It's really weird, but one of my favorite positions to read in is upside down in a rocking chair," claimed Cleo. She told me that regularly, together in the living room, family members sat in silence as each was alone within their book worlds.

When Cleo was not reading in her leisure time, she wrote poetry. She described her home writing as better writing: "I do some stuff for language arts because we have to do that. And I think most of my good stuff that I'm thinking of sending away was just working at home." Cleo regarded herself as a writer, considered a career in writing, and struggled to stretch her reading and writing, unassisted by teachers, whom she found too willing to celebrate rather than critique. She said:

> 'Cause like teachers they think it's wonderful and everything, but sometimes it doesn't seem right. Mr. Stone [her sixth-grade teacher] thought all mine were so great last year, and then I would come home, and my mom would criticize it and point out all the stuff that was wrong. So if I got a little more input, it would be better. I like it when people tell you it's sort of good, and then they tell you what's wrong with it.

Throughout the year, a major tension emerged in Cleo's construction of literacy training at home and at school. True to her cookie script, she maintained, as stated earlier, "If anybody gives me an idea, I reject it. It has to be my own"; yet she desired "a little more input." Denying outside influence was central to how Cleo perceived of her role as a reader, a writer, a student, and a human being. It annoyed her greatly when people made suggestions for her literate choices. She rejected their opinions and most often made contrary choices to maintain her role as an independent learner. She openly ignored input from parent, peer, or teacher; yet she criticized teachers for being too easy on her with their praise. On the other hand, on several occasions Cleo complained that her mother was too critical:

> My mom criticizes my writing and says, "Oh, this should be dah, dah, dah, dah." When I wrote this story *Taffy* and my mom told me to be more descriptive, and so I got really mad at her, and I wrote this whole big description and then I go, "Is this good enough?"

She later acknowledged that it was her own anger that produced better writing. All the while, she openly longed for critique and for writing companions. One day she stated, "I wish I had someone to share my writing with," but later in the same interview she said, "I write what I want. Nobody gives me ideas. I write for myself." Her tough-cookie script demanded she go it alone, but her drive to become a writer demanded an audience.

When she received a rejection from *Merlyn's Pen*, a national magazine of student writing that publishes the writing of seventh through tenth graders, she called me to ask what the editor had meant by his comment that she should ground her poem in concrete experiences. She then immediately set to work revising the poem in a manner suggested by the editor. While she admitted that she cried when she received the rejection, she later considered it a turning point in her writing development. "It's like at that moment, I really took off." After her rejection from *Merlyn's Pen*, Cleo became more committed to her writing. She began scouring the school library for poetry-writing books and anthologies.

At the beginning of this study, Cleo described her writing processes as "what just flows out of you," and "it just flows out like a stream." Revision for Cleo was a process of proofreading, of correcting surface errors. Prewriting was internal processing: "I don't plan ahead. I just write it," she said. Whatever landed on the page remained on the page. A final copy was a clean and neatly written replicate of the first draft. Her rejection from *Merlyn's Pen* led her to a different process. She began checking out library books, seeking advice for writing style and possible publications. She praised *Gonna Make Me a Rainbow Poem* and *Getting the Knack* as two key sources that helped her write better. Her drafts became messier. She literally cut and taped drafts together. She sought response from writing textbooks and adults.

Cleo came to understand a close connection between reading and writing with the help of poetry-writing books. She saw a connection between text and audience. In the fall, she said, "I write poetry, but I never read any. I don't like reading poetry because it's too hard to understand.'' In the spring, she turned to texts and anthologies in order to examine the styles of poets.

Cleo used reading for multiple purposes: to escape from her surroundings, to model writing techniques, and to find information in texts. As a writer she encountered more struggles: Her desire to go it alone conflicted with her desire to become a published writer. She turned to texts and turned to her mother, but she did not turn to people available in the school context. A refusal to disclose a vulnerable side of herself in school did not allow Cleo to share her poetry within the language arts class. Only after receiving an acceptance letter from *Merlyn's Pen*, securing her role as a competent, successful writer, did she bring her poetry to school. Perhaps it was the recognition from outside authority that granted her permission to share as a published writer, removing the obstacles of her conceived role as ''impeccable intellect.''

One of Cleo's poems hints at the tensions just beneath the surface, tensions pulling at Cleo's attempts to become a writer—tensions between the public (perfect) and private (vulnerable) selves; between a need to protect her privacy and autonomy and her need for public audiences. Her role as an independent student constricted her ability to turn to those at school, where she conceived a role for herself as flawless because ''this is what other people expect.'' Distinct from popular girls, Cleo felt little in common with those at school. Beyond her unwillingness to exhibit vulnerability, Cleo did not perceive herself as inhabiting the same world as most of her peers at school.

In spite of Cleo's feeling of separateness from most teenagers, she occasionally hinted her desires to fulfill the role of a teenager. In the following poem, written as Cleo worked through the exercises in *Getting the Knack*, she wanted to be a teenager; yet notice that, for Cleo, the teenager in this poem remains set in her home.

A Teenager's Room
A teenager's room has a desk drawer open,
   papers falling out.
A teenager's room has Pepsi cans hidden
   from view and closets with hangers
   poking out here and there.
A teenager's room has an overflowing garbage
   container and stuffed animals tumbling
   over empty margarine tubs and jelly jars.
A teenager's room has clothes strewn everywhere
   and unmade beds with sheets pushed off to
   one side.
A teenager's room is activity, bustle and weariness.

> A teenager's room is private so don't go in
>   and kidnap the bit of seclusion they own.
> Please don't.

Never in our conversations did Cleo describe herself as a teenager; yet, in this poem, Cleo explored the role. Most often she rejected any notion of adolescence and saw herself as very distinct from girls she described as "popular blonde girls" and "bubble-headed girls."

Her literate practices, it seems, were chosen to present herself as more adult. For example, she often selected books from *the New York Times* Best Seller List and never carried R. L. Stine books to class, although her mother told me that she read them on occasion. She also, on rare occasions, picked up a Christopher Pike book belonging to her younger sister. However, the books she carried to her language arts class were used to document her high literary standards. She carried Shakespeare, *A Wrinkle in Time*, and titles from the best-seller lists, showcasing her more adult literary tastes.

During my year of data collection, despite multiple invitations and prompts from teachers, Cleo did not cross friendship boundaries. Her allegiances created barriers. Throughout the entire seventh-grade year, I observed only one literate artifact in which these firm borders were crossed, a note from Cleo to Tiffany. The note follows:

> Tiffany,
> This is a game of romance since 1847. Copy this letter word for word 7 times and give it to 7 different people (no guys) within 4 days. Copy this by hand! This is not a joke! It has worked for years. On the 4th day drink a glass of milk and say a guy's name and on the 6th day, he will ask you out. If you break the chain, you will have bad luck with boys forever. This starts when you read this note! Remember this is not a joke! Cleo Houser

Cleo explained to me why she had written to Tiffany: "You're pretty much desperate to find someone to send them to. You have to find people that haven't gotten one." The promise of romance coupled with the threat of having "bad luck with boys forever" broke through firm social networks and well-established social roles, something teachers were unable to do.

SCHOOL-SANCTIONED LITERACIES

The tough cookies always did every assignment on time. They were never late. Although they may have complained about the boring, stupid, or senseless nature of some assignment, they were extremely thorough and serious with each one. They did not ask for help from each other. If Dottie needed help, she freely turned to her mother or her teacher. On several occasions, she called her teacher in the evening to ensure that her work was correct. It seems understandable, then, that her teacher didn't see her as self-reliant. Cleo, on the other hand, did not ask for help.

Just as they felt cast into roles by the construction of the classroom, the cookies held each teacher firmly to his or her teacherly role. Dottie remarked one day about the difference between sixth grade and seventh grade. "It's like last year they were teachers. This year they are teacher-teachers." For her, "teacher-teachers" distanced themselves. Dottie and Cleo explained the distinction between teachers and teacher-teachers in this way:

DOTTIE: I mean, at Parkview almost all of the teachers had a personality.
CLEO: And they acted like they cared about you, really.
DOTTIE: And what was important was your homework, not if you got in the door on time.
CLEO: And they were concerned about you.
DOTTIE: This year it's different. I liked it better last year.

From the perspective of the cookies, junior high teachers were more interested in rules than they were in students. They were stricter and less willing to share stories about themselves and their families. The girls perceived junior high teachers' roles as giving out and collecting assignments. The cookies admitted that some teachers were bad, describing a bad teacher as one who did not give clear directions or articulate expectations for grading. In another interview, the cookies' sense of a teacher's role became clearer. After I returned from a national conference, Cleo asked me about my trip. When I relayed the fact that I had read two poems to an informal audience, Cleo asked, "Did they respond like a teacher?" Asked to elaborate, she explained, "Did they correct it?" Despite their language arts teachers' lengthy written and oral comments filled with praise and questions of content, the role of the writing teacher was considered to be that of a corrector of errors, little else.

Current assumptions about sound writing pedagogy privilege social interactions as the centerpiece; yet, for Cleo and Dottie, social interactions in the school setting were often considered an invasion of privacy; as Dottie regularly expressed, "It's none of their business." Drawing on his writing project training, Rick Tibidioux, her teacher, often designed writing prompts for their daily journals in which students were asked to write about their personal experiences. During the first week of school, for example, he asked students to write how their lives had changed in the last month. Students shared their trips to the mall to buy new school clothes and their last summer excursions. Dottie did not share what she had written about her father putting their dogs to sleep because he had recently lost his job, and they could no longer afford to feed them.

The following transcripts reflect the tensions that created obstacles for writing instruction:

DOTTIE: They [teachers] ask you for a nice, clean copy and then they mark it all up. They ruin it.

CLEO: I hate it when you have to share ideas in a group. People can steal your ideas. If anyone gives me an idea, I have to reject it. It has to be mine.

M.F.: What about when your teacher writes on the side of your paper and says, "How about this?"

DOTTIE: I hate that. I mean when you have a polished copy, and you did your best, and then there's slobber all over it.

M.F.: Slobber?

DOTTIE: Yeah, right on it, and then you don't have your own paper anymore.

CLEO: Yeah, on those research papers that we did last year. They looked so nice, and then the teachers write all over them. Yeah, like they make corrections and then—[Dottie interrupts.]

DOTTIE: Yeah, like my John Wayne thing. It was perfectly fine until Mr. Stone corrected it.

CLEO: Half the time. Well at least he didn't write it in RED!

DOTTIE: Some teachers circle.

CLEO: They could write on the back at least.

DOTTIE: They circle all the mistakes, and when you get it back, all you see is these little circles.

M.F.: What about when they write good things on it? When they tell you how much they like something?

CLEO: It's annoying.

DOTTIE: That's what I hate.

CLEO: They should TELL you. And they should give you a comment sheet, you know, and we could keep it in our red folder [school writing folders].

DOTTIE: If they want to write comments, they can and not ruin your work.

CLEO: It's really rude. They mess up your work.

DOTTIE: Yeah, and sometimes the pen leaks and stuff and makes blobs.

M.F.: Do you think teachers could mark on some things and not others?

CLEO: First drafts.

DOTTIE: Yeah, first drafts, but your polished copies, your final drafts, they should leave them blank.

M.F.: I know you have been spending a lot of time in your classes responding to each other's work. Do you like that? Do you find that useful?

DOTTIE: Sometimes, sometimes it's private. It's personal. I don't like other people to see it. The reason why teachers have you correct each other's papers is so they don't have to check like 300 of them.

M.F.: I don't mean the correction part. I mean when others read and respond to your work.

DOTTIE: Well when it's personal stuff, I don't want it. I just say Joanie, I'll put it in my different handwriting and sign Joanie's name. Sometimes it's nobody's business, and Mr. Tibidioux will say, "Ah, pass it to your neighbor."

Embedded throughout this transcript are themes that interfere with literacy instruction as envisioned by the teachers. Those literate practices that worked against the school sanctions were constructed not as acts of resistance but rather a means of self-protection. Literate underlife protected the cookies from self-disclosure. Protection from self-disclosure worked against the social interactions that have come to dominate current writing pedagogy. As Dottie revealed, when she was asked to share private writing, she had learned to protect herself from disclosure by writing a response to her own writing in a contrasting ink and signing another student's name. Notice, too, the sense of loss of ownership when someone attempts to influence the writing.

Also missing was the connection between audience and writer. The cookies held with a notion of revision as correction of errors, even when the structure of the class was designed for response groups. Going it alone as the central driving theme in the cookies' scripts worked against sanctioned literacy instruction.

Cookies did their very best, but best was accomplished alone, uninfluenced by others. Drawing from the discourse of adolescence, teachers most often assumed that junior high students found working with same-age peers valuable and comfortable, thus privileging group work. In different language arts classes, the cookies resisted working in groups, and they found sharing their writing with others to be extremely unproductive. The message "take care of yourself" was carried into such group interactions.

They referred to sharing ideas as "cheating" and "stealing." They looked for, and found, ways to successfully bypass group projects and interactions. In Dottie's class, for example, her teacher required daily journal entries with a signed written response from a classmate. The intention of the teacher was evident in his mini-lessons on response. He directed the students to respond productively and positively, emphasizing explicitly the need for an audience and the importance of a positive writing community.

For the first week, Dottie sat, taking a long time to decide whether to cooperate or rebel, choosing either on any particular day. The sense of community that the teacher was working to build early in the year was oppositional to Dottie's view that "it's none of their business." She soon began changing pens and writing a response to herself in a different color ink from the entry. Holding open her journal, she explained the process to me, "See, I just change my handwriting and write 'Bye, Rachel.'" This practice was not considered rule-breaking by Dottie, who viewed it as a means to protect her privacy.

Like Dottie, Cleo resented being asked to work with others. She explained:

> I would prefer to never work in groups. I don't like it, and it is obvious to me that I'm in groups with the bad kids. And I'm there to keep them in line. And I don't want to be their babysitter, and I know that is what teachers want me to be, but I don't want to be the babysitter. Look at what they expect you to do in a group! They are really individual activities, and you just have to divide up the jobs. The others never do their share and I just end up doing it all.

Cleo did not see any value in sharing with peers. From her perspective, there was no sense of collaborative work; rather, "They are really individual activities." In another interview she said of her social studies class, "The teacher's idea is to put us in groups, and then I give the answers to the other kids who didn't do the work. That's cheating!"

One can see that such perceptions of groups run counter to most currently accepted pedagogical approaches. If one accepts the Vygotskian notion that students learn best in the presence of experts or more capable peers (Vygotsky, 1978), one can see how deeply problematic the issue becomes in a classroom where a teacher might view working together as sound pedagogy, while some students view such practices as "cheating and stealing." Such sound pedagogy violated the cookies' sense of protection of their private world.

Dottie and Cleo remained true to their tough-cookie script, vehemently denying ever receiving any help on school projects. Because one of my driving assumptions was that peer groups would become more influential at this particular developmental stage, I often asked each girl about who had suggested a writing topic, a particular book selection, where ideas had come from. Although as Bakhtin (1981) suggests, words come "out of other people's mouths," the cookies considered any borrowing bad. The cookies did not acknowledge influence and believed that they could and did own ideas singularly. The following conversation illustrates the strong sense of singular ownership:

M.F.: Why did you select all these titles? [I show Cleo the list of all books that she has checked out of the school library over the year.] Some of them I know were for particular classes, but anything in particular that led you to some of these?

CLEO: I just look and find something I like and a topic I'm interested in.

M.F.: Anybody suggest books for you?

CLEO: Not really.

M.F.: Who do you talk to about books when you're reading?

CLEO: Nobody.

M.F.: When and where do you do most of your reading?

CLEO: Probably at home.

M.F.: Do you think anything or anyone influenced your selection of reading?

CLEO: No.

M.F.: Any ideas ever come from TV or friends?

CLEO: Not really.

Cookies insisted consistently throughout the year that nobody had given them any ideas. Each idea, each choice, each decision was their own, and they hadn't stolen it from anywhere. For example, when asked, "What do you think influences your book selections most?" Cleo answered, "Nothing. I just pick up a book and read it." Her answer echoed the values of her mother, who answered the same question privately five months earlier: "I don't know. Whatever you happen to pick up. Whatever hits you."

There was consistent evidence of ventriloquation, the process by which one voice speaks through another (Bakhtin, 1981); yet, when I asked who influenced a particular reading or writing practice, the response echoed that same insistence on singular performance. Dottie insisted, "Who chooses books for me? Nobody. I choose my own books." Dottie explained her reading and writing selection processes in this way:

DOTTIE: Well, I looked at the cover, and I read just a couple pages, and it was like, some parts of it were mysteries. And if I don't read or look at the cover, then I won't get it.

M.F.: Do you talk to anybody about the things you're reading?

DOTTIE: No. Except for you.

M.F.: Did you talk to anybody about your writing?

DOTTIE: No, only except my mom. I had her look over it, any mis-spelled words or anything. She was about the only one who read it.

M.F.: And how did you go about thinking about making changes?

DOTTIE: Well, some, I reread it and looked at the story, and some parts of it then didn't sound right, so then I re-changed that to make it more interesting.

M.F.: You didn't have anybody read it and give you advice on it before that?

DOTTIE: Well, mom. That was the only person. My sister didn't help with that.

Noticing what was present as well as what was absent in the above transcript, it became clear that, for Dottie, peer groups were not influential. When pushed to name anyone who might have helped with her writing, Dottie did not mention peer groups but, rather, her mother and sister.

At a conscious level, Cleo consistently resisted acknowledging any influence. If questions were framed to avoid direct statements of influence, however, she revealed a subconscious sense of support. The following quote is from the same interview in which Cleo insisted that nobody gave her ideas:

M.F.: Tell me about this gym teacher [the subject of a story she had written].

CLEO: Okay. My mom gave me the idea for that because she had this very strict gym teacher when she was younger, when she lived in Idaho and she would make you do all the work and stuff and make you do how she wanted it done, and she taught science, too. So, when my mom described her that just gave me the idea 'cause I needed something to write about.

While it was apparent that both Cleo and Dottie were influenced by others, especially those at home, they maintained claims to the contrary. Behaviors influenced by others signaled weakness or—worse—might be construed as "kissing up," which carried with it an implicit assumption that one was working to please another rather than oneself.

In one interview, Cleo expressed concerns that made it perfectly clear that she was not a kiss-up. Her grades, she emphasized, were based on her academic work, not on her ability to work with others:

> You know how I would never kiss up? [She looks to Dottie for affirmation.] Right, Dottie? I never kiss up. Well, this one time I wanted to tell the teacher that I liked him, but that's not kissing up because I really thought so. Now, if you tell anyone this I will kill you. Dottie is the only one who knows, and I don't want anyone to think I would kiss up *for any reason*.

From the cookies' perspective, kissing up was a fraudulent practice. In opposition to teacher-pleasing behaviors, Cleo wanted to make it perfectly clear that her actions were independent actions based on her goals and her needs. She did not compromise "for any reason," enunciating the words with firmness to emphasize the seriousness of the claim. Kissing up was one of the most extreme infractions of independent actions. The cookies regarded kissing up, cheating and stealing, and sharing in the classroom as violations of independent action, all viewed as obstacles to be avoided rather than as opportunity.

In contrast, their language arts teachers held quite different assumptions about appropriate practices. Sharing was central to their pedagogy, regarded as a critical link in establishing a reading/writing community. In addition to sharing, each of the teachers articulated the necessity of designing a curriculum built on "free choice." Yet, as has been evident throughout this study, there was no free choice. Personal choices were entangled with social relations. Choices carried heavy costs in terms of expectations, entitlements, and consequences from competing social networks.

For example, Cleo regularly expressed to me her desire to write what she called "issues papers," explained as "essays in which you expressed your opinion on an important issue," yet for writing workshop she wrote narratives. She did not write one opinion paper. Her stories for language arts were almost exclusively personal narratives with the addition of a few poems. Throughout the year, she expressed privately to me her desire to write about issues as they had been assigned in her sixth-grade language arts class.

While Mrs. Zmoleck regularly invited students to write whatever they wanted, Cleo held a narrow definition of appropriate subjects and structures. In class, she did not write about what most interested her: women's rights, gun control, or animal protection. From her perspective, these were not valid choices. She was constricted by her tightly held definition of workshop writing as narrative. While she was willing to mark herself as an outsider in her dress and in the books she carried, her tightly conceived notion of what counted as writing limited her in the writing workshop atmosphere.

As a sixth-grader, Cleo wrote a deeply felt piece about women's rights, a topic that had been assigned. While the piece was well received by her sixth-grade teacher and many of the sixth graders, in seventh grade she was still on occasion referred to as "the one who wrote that woman lib stuff last year." I heard such comments made to her during passing time between classes and occasionally during lunch. Now more constrained by their roles as adolescents, tied to the romantic aspects of being teenagers, the same girls who had praised the piece in sixth grade ridiculed her in seventh grade. Haunting her for over a year, this one piece of writing about women's rights may have limited her ability to compose another issues piece. Her seventh-grade peers on multiple occasions reminded her of the consequences of becoming "that women's lib girl." A teacher's assignment, granting it sanction, might have "freed" Cleo of the social consequences of which she was reminded in the hallways, in study hall, on the bus, and at lunch.

In a final exit interview, I questioned Cleo about her desire for the teacher to assign a topic and her resistance to teacher directives.

M.F.: Something that I've heard you saying over and over again is that you wish Mrs. Zmoleck had made specific assignments, given specific composition assignments instead of free choice. Do you feel that way now?

CLEO: Yeah, I mean she pretty much let you write whatever you wanted. I mean we never did anything with essays.

M.F.: Is that what you would change if you could?

CLEO: More writing assignments that ask you to state your opinion. Not about a book but about an issue.

M.F.: But you could have done that.

CLEO: No. If you have an assignment then you have to write about it.

Notice that Cleo did not perceive Mrs. Zmoleck's invitations to write "whatever you want" to include writing about issues. The interview continued:

M.F.: But you said that you didn't like writing assignments, that were "too assigned" and "too structured" and you didn't like it. So it seems to me that you are saying that you do, and you don't, want assignments.

CLEO: Well, it's like a specific format to it. You know, and if we asked her to give us just an assignment or something we could do anything we wanted with it, we could mess around with it and stuff. And we would just have a topic to write off of. Also, if we just had the topic to write off of, it would be all the same thing, but it wouldn't have every line assigned. And it wouldn't be a composition.

M.F.: So in a composition you would like her to assign a topic and not a form. Either a topic or say write about an issue. And then you would have to state your opinion about it. I've noticed that most everything you write is fictional.

CLEO: It's what you're supposed to write.

Constrained by her role as a model student and haunted by the enduring reception of one piece of writing, Cleo did not have "free choice" in the classroom. Her assumptions about teachers' expectations limited her choices even further. Such social consequences of the workshop classroom created obstacles of which teachers were, for the most part, unaware.

Because it was a common practice in Mr. Tibidioux's class for students to respond to the written work of other students, he taught response directly as a way to, as he said, "build a classroom community. Students share their ideas, and then they really come together." After time had been allocated for writing, Mr. Tibidioux asked students to exchange papers and write a written response to each other's work. As noted earlier, Dottie did not always follow these directives and chose to write a response to herself in a different color ink. On one particular occasion in which Dottie did choose to participate, her response did not bring her into the classroom community but rather marked her as an outsider. A poem about how much one boy wanted to see the Chicago White Sox baseball team play was displayed on the student writing bulletin board across the back of the classroom. Dottie's response set her up for ridicule within the social networks in the classroom. Her response, which she stapled to the poem, read:

Jay, I agree with you. I love sports. I've never been to a football game or anything, but I would like to too. Your friend, Dottie Walters.

In an attempt to align herself with her peers, she unknowingly marked herself as an outsider lacking knowledge of football and baseball teams, knowledge that carried much currency within popular, powerful social networks. Additional comments from other students added later to the White Sox poem parodied her words, "Hey, Jay, I like basketball too" and "Duh, I like football. *Your* friend!"

Clearly, while Dottie and Cleo were succeeding within the school sanctions, they were very much considered outsiders by themselves and by other students.

SUMMARY AND CONCLUSIONS

In summary, the cookies privileged individuality over group membership; thus, they denied allegiance even when influence from others was evident in their daily routines. Since the cookies' reason for being at school was located primarily in the academic realm, school-sanctioned literacies were perceived as a direct route to academic as well as economic success; yet, the need to appear in control and successful prevented the sharing of uncertainties or vulnerabilities.

From the perspective of the cookies, only two social roles were available within the school context: individuals able to take care of themselves and those influenced by peers. The first was desired, the second avoided. Because of their long personal histories as autonomous, the cookies constructed literacy as a singular endeavor and struggled with conflicting personal needs and public expectations.

In review, common themes in literacy events emerged: (1) Literacy is a solitary act; (2) literacy is used to deny allegiance; (3) tensions arise between the needs to protect the private self and the necessity of public performances. The cookies used literacy as a tool to mark one as independent. Group work that demanded collaboration was often coopted, as was response to individual papers. Solidarity and allegiance were most often denied. A desire for solitude was the norm.

For the cookies there were two kinds of writing: "for the teacher or for me." This division was a distinction between texts that were assigned within the school context and texts for private purposes. The school as public arena demanded adherence to sanctioned practices in order to achieve success, and that success was regarded as an individual accomplishment. Reading and writing "for me" was private and often guarded to protect one from self-disclosure. The cookies did not share what they considered their best writing with their teachers, most often because they considered it personal and private business. Distinctions between the public and private created obstacles in the classroom. Other studies agree that for working-class females a public–private dichotomy exists and emphasize the importance of the private (Weiss, 1993). Cleo began to struggle with the distinction that she had held. Dottie, on the other hand, maintained the division and continued to rip up her papers when she finished writing them.

The connectedness that each cookie felt to her mother dominated conversations and observations; yet, assumptions transported from the discourse of adolescence that all adolescents seek membership within same-age peer groups denied much of their lived experience. When the cookies aligned themselves with their mothers, such practices marked them as outsiders at the junior high. Lauren, for example, commented about the cookies: "Of course, they get good grades. They don't do anything. They don't go anywhere. They just stay home on Saturday night and REEEAD!" Even teachers' friendly references to such things as Friday-night football games, drama club tryouts, school yearbooks, or upcoming dances did not match their lived experiences.

As these 12- and 13-year-old girls entered junior high, they faced a new cultural scene with new rules and rituals. Competing roles created obstacles and tensions as the cookies negotiated between the home and the school. Contrasts between the two contexts appeared greater on entry into junior high. Mothers and daughters talked more about loss than gain during this transitional period. The greatest loss felt was the loss of connectedness to adults. Because of the loss of school connectedness, Cleo's family moved away during the summer after her seventh-grade year. Although their trailer remained unsold, they left Northern Hills Community Schools in order to enroll Cleo in a tiny rural school where, her mother hoped, "Teachers might know her better."

Shaped by the discourse of adolescence, the actions of school personnel, the structure of the junior high school, and the language arts curriculum betrayed the cookies, blinding all to the diverse needs of these individuals. Teachers who had been their allies in sixth grade abandoned them in junior high. Peer-group associations were stripped away. Without connections, they struggled to succeed, and they did.

CHAPTER 5

Viewing and Reviewing Classroom Roles

The rolling hills and rich farmland on the mural at the entrance to the junior high building portrayed a safe haven, the same kind of environment that teachers at Northern Hills worked so hard to cultivate. Just as fences and bridges impose a kind of orderliness on the landscape, so too do schedules and classroom walls seek to hold off the dynamic flow of students' lives. At Northern Hills, teachers talked of classrooms as "safe havens" and "nurturing environments," creating filters that deflected attention away from the dynamic swirl of competing expectations and allegiances that attend early adolescence. Classrooms viewed as autonomous provide a hold against rich complexities, and curriculum guides designed for orderly progression impose order on such chaos. A classroom door is closed in order to keep out the swirl of movement, yet we must work within that dynamism rather than deny it.

As this study unfolded, an uneasiness began to grow in me about terms that I had found quite comfortable in my 13 years of teaching language arts in a junior high school. I had never questioned terms such as "ownership," "community," and "collaboration." "Adolescence" and "student-centered pedagogy" became visible as what Burke (1990) called "terministic screens." He explained how language works like photographic lenses to filter reality, deflecting attention away from the rich complexities of students' lived experiences and creating a lens too narrow to view the power of the social dynamic. Quite willing to problematize the notion of the autonomous self, I nonetheless held to a pedagogy that did little to take into account the self as situated in a complex web of social relations.

I selected Northern Hills as the research site because I knew and valued highly the teachers and the pedagogy that they embraced. As a supervisor of student teachers at a nearby university, I had the opportunity to observe this department in action on multiple occasions. I facilitated a summer writing project for this district and often said that this would be the finest place to teach anywhere in the nation. The philosophy and atmosphere matched what I valued; yet after one year of documenting the literate lives of some of the adolescent girls who attended Northern Hills, I am less sure of the pedagogy that I had so completely embraced.

What can be drawn from our deepened understanding of the lived experiences of these Euro-American females growing up in the rural Midwest, girls who by most measures are succeeding in school, girls who will most likely continue to succeed?

I contend that it is neither an individual moving through identifiable stages of development in a linear, predictable fashion, nor an individual welcomed into a harmonious community that prompts learning. Rather, it is within the complex weave of social relations that students learn. It is like the ripping apart of fabrics from old clothes and stitching them back together into some new, yet familiar patchwork pattern, designing one's own quilt in which the patches are neither static nor distinct. As children sever old ties and make new connections, turning away from childhood's roles toward adult identities, the teaching and learning of appropriate literate behaviors play an important role in this complex social negotiation.

RENDERING VISIBLE "TERMINISTIC SCREENS"

The discourse that we accept defines us and shapes our relationships to others. Through this study two discourses became visible: the discourse of student-centered pedagogy and the discourse of adolescence. Entangled together, each reinforced the other, normalizing a particular way of being in junior high school.

Entry into seventh grade comes as one is entering adolescence. The philosophy on which the junior high was constructed emerged from the discourse of adolescence: hence, the discourse of adolescence coupled with the structure and schedule of the junior high school may work against understanding the diversity of adolescence. Most often, understanding of the historical, economic, social, and cultural complexities that shape the lives of adolescents disappears.

Teachers' roles, like students' roles, remain constrained by an unquestioned embrace of a discourse, a discourse rendered transparent by our familiarity with it. Classrooms hold certain expectations that are rarely made explicit and rarely called into question. Close examination reveals several myths within the discourse.

MYTHS OF STUDENT-CENTERED PEDAGOGY

Gaining fluency by writing in a risk-free environment and connecting reading and writing to one's personal background are commonly articulated as the foundation of a language arts pedagogy. Nancie Atwell (1987), who may be considered the leading authority of middle school literacy pedagogy, describes the teacher's role in the following manner: "When we sit quietly, wait and listen, our students will tell us what they're trying to do as writers. Our job is to give time and ownership, and then help them know what it is they want to use time to do" (p. 65). Clearly, from Tiffany, Lauren, Angie, Cleo and Dottie, we have learned that giving time and ownership is not enough.

Throughout this study, the girls' perceptions of the social consequences of their actions directly affected their classroom behaviors. Social roles beyond the classroom directly influence those within. Yet, the discourse of student-centered pedagogy creates filters that hide the contamination of the classroom by other contexts and other social roles.

The Myth of a Safe Haven

Classroom walls are perceived as somehow capable of holding out other dimensions of students' lives. While many teachers may admit that establishing a safe haven is elusive, it is most often held up as a noble goal. I would argue that such a goal is both impossible and undesirable. Such a goal renders the political charge surrounding a classroom neutral. It denies disparate positions of power in the classroom and in the larger culture.

Despite teachers' perceptions of the success of small-group work and reading/writing workshops, the girls, constrained by their social roles, coopted literate practices when forced to work with those outside their circle of significance; yet, they maintained the appearance of performing in socially sanctioned ways. The only bit of evidence I saw in which the queens and the cookies crossed friendship lines was a series of chain letters that promised romance and threatened balkers with "bad luck with boys forever."

From the perspectives of the focal students, literate practices could be unsafe. Carrying the wrong kind of book, writing the wrong kind of story, passing notes to the wrong people, all might mark one as an outsider or as an insider in the wrong group. Tiffany and Angie maintained their social status by borrowing and buying stories. Even within their stories, particular students held center stage, maintaining alle-

giances to a popular crowd and marginalizing others who did not popu-
late their texts. Like the queens, Cleo and Dottie carried books to maintain a distinction from other groups. They did not carry R. L. Stine
books to class. They refused to share work in groups, and refused to
expose vulnerabilities. The focal students were all keenly aware of the
social consequences of their classroom actions. Being accused of "kissing up," for example, held different repercussions for different peer
networks.

Indeed, there were multiple expectations circulating about the junior high classroom. As has been evident throughout this study, the
institutional expectations, while clearly understood by the focal students, were often coopted by the girls in order to meet the expectations
of other social networks. A keen awareness of the power of peer dynamics in the classroom prevented any student from believing in a classroom
as a safe haven.

The Myth of Comfort

Built into the creation of the classroom as a safe haven is the notion
that comfort will empower students to take risks that lead to learning.
Teachers at Northern Hills worked to "make students feel comfortable." Mr. Tibidioux envisioned his classroom as a place in which students "feel comfortable to share their ideas." But for Dottie, comfort
was rare. She fought against self-disclosure. She protected her thoughts
by writing responses to herself. Silences within this discourse disregard
the political power wielded by some students at the expense of others.

A pedagogy built on comfort, built on students' experiences, will,
of course, continue to privilege those who feel most at home in the
classroom. Throughout this study, those students who appeared to feel
most comfortable, whose voices were loudest and quickest, were those
who were generally regarded by their peers as holding popular power.
Such power was attained through physical appearance, socioeconomic
status, and athletic prowess—attributes all gained beyond the classroom
walls.

For the most part, students at Northern Hills appeared to me to be
far too comfortable with their work and with their perspectives. Little
change was observed over the course of the year. How much comfort is
too much comfort? Lloyd-Jones described his job as a teacher in this
way: "It's the sand in the oyster. You don't want to have so much sand
that you kill the oyster, but you want enough to have a pearl every now
and then" (quoted in Finders, 1992, p. 507).

The Myth of Inclusion

Characterized as "communities," classrooms were perceived as capable of holding out conflicting dimensions of students' lives. Mr. Tibidioux taught specific response strategies in order to build a sense of shared community. After time had been allocated for writing, Mr. Tibidioux asked students to exchange papers and write a written response to each other's work. As noted earlier, Dottie did not always follow these directives and chose to write a response to herself in a different color ink. On one particular occasion in which Dottie chose to participate, her response did not bring her into the classroom community but rather marked her as an outsider. Lacking knowledge that carried currency within the classroom community, Dottie documented an absence of shared culture.

The Myth of Free Choice

Perhaps the greatest myth of all is the assumption that students' choices can be choices free from sociopolitical tangles. Awareness of political and social consequences limited choices for the cookies and the queens. "Free choices" were not free from the webs of social relationships. Throughout the year, I heard Mrs. Zmoleck and Mr. Tibidioux invite students to choose freely what they read and wrote; yet, students could not accept such invitations.

Students' selection criteria were tied to their social roles and filtered through their literate histories as students, daughters, and friends. The girls all made metered choices that took into account their roles and relationships in competing social networks. Tiffany, for example, although very interested in the novel *The Cay*, was not free to conform to the role of good student. Likewise, very committed to women's rights, Cleo did not write about feminism or raise such issues during discussions—perhaps because her sixth-grade essay on feminism haunted her throughout her seventh-grade year. When I asked Cleo directly why she wrote personal narratives rather than writing about what mattered to her most, her response was, "It's what you're supposed to write." Likewise, Lauren held a narrow view of what one was supposed to read during sustained silent reading and did not choose to read sports books.

Despite invitations from their teachers to read and write whatever they chose, all of the girls in this study understood reading and writing workshop time as time to read and write fiction and personal narratives. Focal students considered expressive writing and narrative writing to be

what the teachers valued as "good writing." Angie directly told
me, "It's what you have to write. It's the only thing they [teachers]
count."

MYTHS OF ADOLESCENCE

The period of adolescence is for the most part characterized as biologically determined, with little consideration for any social or cultural influences. The view that adolescence is a period of storm and stress persists,
with hormonal factors often accounting for the marked fluctuations in
adolescent behaviors (Brooks-Gunn & Reiter, 1990). Coleman's (1961)
landmark study led to a construction of adolescence as a subculture
sharply distinct from adult culture. Such a view of adolescent has led to
the construction of the adolescent as a singular identity.

The Myth of the Universal Adolescent

The adolescent is understood as a somewhat generic entity. The homogeneity that pervades the discourse of adolescence denies how one is
socially, perhaps idiosyncratically constituted. The needs of the adolescent are generally regarded as universal needs, most often characterized
as needs for greater autonomy, more activities with same-age peers, and
greater distance from adults.

Throughout this study, we have seen multiple and competing influences that shape how one enters adolescence. From the cookies and the
queens we have learned that despite outward signs of homogeneity,
diversity shapes how one embarks on the journey toward adulthood.
Adolescence, then, cannot be examined without regard to race, class, or
gender. Further, from Dottie and Cleo we learn that one's experiential
background further diversifies beyond race, class, and gender.

The Myth of Adolescence as a Negative Period

Adolescence is generally regarded as an inherently negative period
filled with "storm and stress." In contrast, at the end of the seventh-
grade year, all mothers reported with relief that their fears of impending
turmoil had not been realized. However, buying into this assumption,
the queens often accentuated their stress through dramatic public performances. On the other hand, stress was often created for the cookies
because they did not fit the pervasive adolescent model.

Teachers often attributed conflicts that arose within the classroom to hormonal factors, conflicts that may have been based on substantive social and political issues. On numerous occasions, I heard comments similar to "That comes with the territory, you know how junior high students are." Indeed, biological changes influenced behaviors of the girls, but such changes in behaviors seemed at times to have been staged in order to match this adolescent assumption. During my year of data collection, Dottie and Cleo both articulated conflicts and tensions that had nothing to do with hormones. Indeed, tensions did exist, but the queens' keen sense of playfulness, frolic, and fun overshadowed their turmoil. Likewise, in their homes, the cookies rarely expressed negativity and exhibited great pleasure in their activities.

The Myth of Severed Ties with Adults

Adolescent culture cannot be located in its opposition to adult culture. Rather than maintaining the false assumption that adolescence is a period of alienation from adults, we should acknowledge and nurture the connectedness that adolescents feel to adults. Clearly, Cleo and Dottie were very much connected to their mothers and longed for closer connections to their teachers.

All of the girls in this study turned to their mothers for guidance and support. While the queens reported a denial of their connections to their parents, the parents remained very much central. On multiple occasions, I observed behaviors that conflicted with their self-reports. Tiffany, for example, spent much time with both her mother and her stepfather. Also, all the queens reported a close tie with Angie's mother. In May of their daughters' sixth-grade year, all mothers expressed concerns for the social changes about to affect their relationships with their daughters. In May of the seventh-grade year, there appeared to be a collective sigh of relief as mothers let go of the fears of losing their daughters completely to peer groups.

The assumption of the necessity of severed ties guides curricular decisions and governs teacher–student interaction patterns. For example, group work in the junior high setting often ignored the complex negotiating necessary because of the assumption that all adolescents desired work with same-age peers. I did not hear Northern Hills teachers question how such an activity might privilege some teens over others. They did, however, recognize obstacles that impeded group work, but generally attributed tensions to the essence of the junior high student.

"THEY'RE ALL GOOD GIRLS": VIEWING CLASSROOM ROLES

Recent gender studies point an accusing finger at schools, citing the limited range of available roles for females (American Association of University Women [AAUW], 1992; Gilligan, 1988; Sadker & Sadker, 1986; Walkerdine, 1990). Evidence from my research supports such claims. Student-centered pedagogy as it was enacted at Northern Hills was built on the prevalent discourse of adolescence. Left unexamined, the myths in the discourse of adolescence constrain the teacher's role as well as students' roles in the classroom. Perceiving entry into adolescence to be a negative period filled with storm and stress, Northern Hills teachers advocated "comfort" as their primary goal for their students.

Metaphors of teacher as nurturer, teacher as facilitator, have normalized the teacher's role that privileges helpfulness. Appropriate behaviors for teachers and girls alike could be described in Walkerdine's (1990) words as "nice, kind and helpful." Teachers at Northern Hills articulated their jobs as facilitating discussions. In my observations throughout the year, teachers orchestrated discussions by inviting students to talk, praising responses, regulating turn-taking, and reprimanding disruptive behavior.

According to Vygotsky (1978), students learn from an expert or more capable peer, but it seems that this notion of the teacher as critical expert has been lost. In current thinking about student-centered pedagogy, most often the teacher's job is reduced to "making students feel comfortable." A growing body of research has begun to critique process-oriented student-centered pedagogy because it does not meet the needs of diverse student populations (Delpit, 1988, 1991; Richardson, 1991). Others point out further limitations (Gilbert, 1988, 1991; Hines, 1992; Kamler, 1993; Walkerdine, 1990), arguing that such a pedagogy denies claims on the social, the cultural, and the ideological, limiting students to consideration of those issues that already exist within their range of experiential knowledge. In other words, students are not stretched beyond their comfort zones. Thus we have reduced possibilities for disrupting the status quo.

This role of the teacher as "nice, kind and helpful" closely matches the traditional role assigned to adult women, that of nurturers (Walkerdine, 1990). Not only are teachers denied opportunities to address issues of social change, but the teacher-as-nurturer role further serves to marginalize the girls in these classrooms. What messages are sent to the young women when teachers privilege "nice, kind, and helpful" over intellectual grappling?

Cleo's mother noticed a similar phenomenon over the years that her daughter had been in public school settings:

> It's like the girls do all the work, and the boys get to star. They [teachers] put Cleo in groups with bad boys 'cause they know she will do all the work. And it's like she has to take care of them. She's supposed to help them do the work. She's supposed to be like their mother or something. But then she has to spend her time getting them to do the work, and it's not fair.

During other interviews, she continued to addressed this concern:

> One time, I asked to see the seating chart because I know they make her [Cleo] sit by the boys because she doesn't get in trouble. . . . She's efficient. Cleo will be all right because she's efficient enough to be used. Teachers tell me that she's good at pacifying a group, holding it all together, keeping boys in line, but I don't want that.

Teachers admitted that this role, described by Judy Houser as "like their [the boys'] mother or something," was a role that they were forced to cast on girls. Language arts teachers at Northern Hills said with regret that the demands of their classrooms forced them to ignore "good girls" and attend to the worst behaviors of particular boys.

On one day in late winter, I sat in the back of Debra Zmoleck's classroom. Students scrambled in as usual. The tardy bell rang and eight seats remained empty. All eight seats were assigned to girls. Debra walked past me and whispered, "I've lost my spacers." She repeated, "I've lost my spacers." I did not understand. She looked down at me and said a third time, "I've lost all my spacers. I know it's terrible to say, but it's true." When I asked her to explain, she said, "Oh, you know: naughty boy, spacer, naughty boy, spacer, naughty boy. It's terrible, but it's what you have to do to survive." I must admit I was taken aback, but I was also taken right back to my years in the public school in which working with 26 young adolescents in 50-minute chunks of time in one room, I too had sometimes resorted to such strategies.

While Mr. Tibidioux did not use such a label, the following quote illustrates that he was using girls for similar purposes:

> I put boys and girls together so they can learn and benefit from each other. Like I put Dottie by Eric. She's timid, and he's high strung. And Angie by Craig. She's sharp and can help him.

So it seems that the institutional design for a good girl positioned her to be used at best as a nurturer and at worst as nothing more than a physical barrier, a "spacer." We understand also what this design does to boys who internalize such gender-specific messages. If girls are nice, kind, and helpful, boys must be the opposite. Boys are taught that disruptive behavior is acceptable male behavior. Boys are taught the role of girls is to serve them.

Viewed in this light, it is hardly surprising that the queens would work to resist such a role. Given the available choices, they broke rules and resisted intellectual engagement in order to fulfill the role of teenagers rather than be seen as girls. The cookies, on the other hand, reported that they resented the available role but complied because of the future benefits it promised.

Where in any of this are students rewarded for intellectual engagement, for wrestling with ideas? I did not observe students ever invited to argue, debate, criticize, or disagree. Docility and deference were privileged. Dissonance was denied.

When one examines the conception of the female student and how that construction has become almost codified, one can more clearly understand how schools reinforce gender stereotypes. I felt throughout my year at Northern Hills that the focal students were clearly trying to find a place at the edge of the good-girl category. Working to avoid disciplinary measures at home, the queens calculated how far beyond the bounds they could go. Likewise, the cookies worked to manipulate the institutional expectations to protect themselves from self-disclosure. We can hardly cast blame on the social queens, who were doing exactly what we have been training girls to do: to find their place in society largely through romance and commodities. Nor can we fault the cookies, who turned to education with the promise that it would help them find a better place in our society.

IMPLICATIONS FOR PEDAGOGY: REVISING OUR ROLES

The complexities of curricular planning for literacy learning become more apparent when one comes to understand the dimensions of multiple and often competing discursive practices. Since learning is enmeshed in social webs, a student-centered curriculum must consider the tangles that constrict students' choices and decisions. I am not suggesting a return to a traditional teacher-centered pedagogy; rather, I am advocating a more explicit examination of the complexities that shape literacy learning, an unmasking of the ways in which social relations and thinking processes impinge on each other.

I advocate a student-negotiated pedagogy with emphasis on the negotiation. Having been a junior high teacher for 13 years, I am not suggesting a move toward open, unbridled conflict in the middle-school classroom, but rather a move toward acknowledging and working within the dynamics that exist there. For instance, I support using such innovations as portfolios not only to broaden students' notions of literacy, but also to make visible the political tensions that accompany literate choices.

Bringing a sociocultural perspective into the middle-school classroom is a beginning. If one were to start with the question "What makes writing good?" from a particular point of view, within a particular set of assumptions, students could puzzle over, wrestle with, and question the answers with growing awareness of multiple perspectives. I advocate explicitly acknowledging the silences and the voices that are motivated by political decisions. For example, examining the social, historical, and cultural motivations of particular roles available—in texts, classrooms, and the larger culture—will lead students to more critical awareness and thus, it is hoped, to the ability to revise those roles. Throughout this study, it is clear that what is missing in a student-centered pedagogy is the necessary addition of layers of critical reflection, an examination of how discourse and the metaphors embedded within it situate individuals.

Students, both male and female, all keenly aware of disparate positions of power, need opportunities to practice dealing with intellectual uncertainties and political tensions. Rather than viewing a class as a safe haven, perhaps it would be more productive to openly articulate the obstacles, barriers, and risks that accompany literacy learning. Students need assistance in this struggle. I advocate bringing dissent into the public arena. Relegated to the background, dissent at Northern Hills Junior High did not promise the possibility of change.

A seventh-grade curriculum might provide a space for what Pratt (1991) calls a "contact zone," a term used to refer to "social spaces where cultures meet, clash, and grapple with each other, often in contexts of highly asymmetrical relations of power" (p. 34). Provided with an arena for critical discussion, students might open up the possibilities for multiple perspectives to be heard and considered. I envision a junior high pedagogy similar to the college composition pedagogy that Miller (1994) describes, in which he expands on Pratt's notion of contact zones by "trying to create a course that allows the students to use their writing to investigate the cultural conflicts that serve to define and limit their lived experience'' (p. 407). Conflicts that defined and limited the roles available to the girls in this study were for the most part ignored or suppressed. Therefore, resistance did not hold promise for revising social expectations. A sociocultural pedagogy must provide students with the tools necessary to examine the powerful constraints that serve to define them.

In looking for solid answers, in seeking stability in this new social arena, the queens and the cookies turned to texts as authoritative. Text served as a "kind of proof," as Angie explained. Texts were rejected or embraced, but there appeared to be no sense of answering back, no critical doubt, no disruption, no tension. There was no sense of a text as dialogic. Unquestioning, Dottie received Home Interiors brochures, just as the queens turned to teen zines. According to Bakhtin (1981), there is a constant struggle between the authoritative and internally persuasive functions of discourse. No such struggle was evident in the classrooms at Northern Hills. Questions designed to open up discussion in the language arts classroom did little to deconstruct the appearance of text as authoritative. Opinion questions for the most part allowed one to embrace or reject a particular text, but permitted no play. How can one expect a critical stance when there is no suggestion of any alternative readings? A sociocultural approach to literacy may provide alternative readings. Students need assistance to expand their range of experiential knowledge, and thus provide possibilities of disrupting the status quo. We can help students learn to ask questions about the political motivations beneath texts. If we ask about the social roles in texts, if we ask questions that cannot be answered by a wholesale embrace or rejection of the text, students will gain necessary practice in uncertainties. I advocate a pedagogy that situates reading not simply as an aesthetic experience but as a political act as well. Moss (1995) challenges existing assumptions about the relationships between texts and readers. She argues that the assumptions that texts are potentially powerful in their effect rest on a notion of vulnerable readers, and that:

> . . . what matters about texts is not the content alone, but the way that content can be mobilized and used by readers. And feminists would expect differences here to be governed, not by randomly individual choice, but by social and collective histories. In other words, we would expect there to be conflicting readings, which could not be settled by reference to the text alone. Rather than attempting to close things down by fixing once and for all what the text means, feminism would fore-ground the social strategies readers bring to the text. (p. 162)

Moss advocates a pedagogical approach that would replace a personal response to reading and "stress the role diverse social and cultural practices play in shaping how texts get read" (p. 163). I strongly agree. Furthermore, a sociocultural approach would place in the foreground both the social strategies that readers bring to the texts *and* what the texts bring to readers. Such a pedagogy would acknowledge the ways in which texts serve to enable and constrain social roles, the ways in which texts tend to normalize particular behaviors.

If we deny our power as educators, we deny our students the opportunity to rewrite cultural and social scripts. The social queens were becoming exactly what marketers have trained them to be, consumers and competitors for men's desires. At age 13, they had few resources or experiences to resist such powerful images. They were vulnerable readers. They appeared to be readily accepting the status quo for young women because they have so few alternative images and no practice in examining text as socially constructed for particular purposes. The cookies, on the other hand, might appear to have resisted the singular role construction for young women, yet they hardly fared better. With neither the economic resources nor the political clout to speak out, they remained silent. While the social queens rehearsed their roles to secure their place in society through romance and commodities, the cookies were reminded again and again that there was no place for them.

IMPLICATIONS FOR FURTHER RESEARCH

Observing early adolescents from the perspective of a teacher, I believed the transition into junior high to be critical in students' literacy development. After spending 13 years with 13-year-olds, I had more questions than answers. At the end of this study, I have more questions still.

Entry into junior high marks a critical juncture in social and cognitive development because of greater emphasis on academics, an increase in expectations for social experiences outside the home, and an intensification of differential gender roles; yet, the dynamics of literacy learning in early adolescence remain severely underresearched. Future studies should expand our understandings of the dynamics of early adolescence and their relationship to literacy learning.

I see a great need to consider further how social-group affiliations constrict and enable particular literate practices, and, most importantly, how pedagogy can break through such networks. Simply stated, I want to know what constitutes a compelling invitation to read or to write. What might that little bit of sand that Lloyd-Jones referred to look like in a middle-school classroom?

Also, further investigation of literate underlife in the school context will hold important implications for pedagogy. As this study progressed, I began to see how our language constructed and constrained entry into adolescence. For example, Mr. Stone, in preparation for their junior high experience, reported to his students, "Next year you'll have much more responsibility for yourself. You won't have some teacher over you telling you what to do. You'll be on your own. You'll have to make your own decisions. You'll have more freedom, but that comes with more responsibility." Parents too warned their daughters: "Next year, you'll be more in charge of yourself" and "When you're in junior high, you'll have a lot more responsibility for yourself." Such rhetoric heightens anticipation. Rhetoric about becoming an adolescent revolves around issues of freedom, independence, and responsibility; yet, for the queens and the cookies, these expectations did not hold true. In junior high, the girls' actual experiences in the school context were constricted time, movement, and talk. Only through literate underlife were these girls provided any opportunity for more freedom, independence, or responsibility. Because movement and contact with friends were so tightly controlled in the junior high setting, underlife provided the only avenue to fulfill the promises offered in the prevailing discourse.

I am especially concerned with exploring the multiple mediational means in operation as teachers and early adolescents negotiate their roles and relationships in the language arts classroom. In light of this study, I am also interested in pursuing research that would explore how connections to significant adults can impact on literacy learning, investigating how teacher education programs can better prepare educators to work with middle-school students and exploring further the critical connection between home and school during this developmental period. Also, research that explores in depth the perspectives of parents as they accompany their children through adolescence holds the promise of adding understanding to this stage of life, and implications for social and educational programs.

This study was limited in that the portion of time spent in sixth grade was not long enough to examine how literacy learning was situated in the self-contained elementary classroom. Comments from parents, teens, and the teacher who moved from sixth grade to seventh grade lead me to believe that many of the tensions exhibited in seventh grade did not exist in sixth grade. Recently, certain middle schools have emerged, which have begun to reconceptualize appropriate schooling for this age group. Longitudinal ethnographic studies set in middle schools will add greatly to our understanding of appropriate schooling for this age group.

Much work is left to be done in gaining understanding of the complexities that shape early adolescence. There exists an urgent need in our society to better serve these young people, not just girls but all students.

JUST GIRLS

The phrase "just girls" echoed throughout interviews and observations during my year at Northern Hills. "Just girls," both the cookies and queens claimed, whenever I pushed them to describe themselves. "Just girls" emerged from the mouths of adolescent boys to dismiss and diminish girls' positions in the classroom.

The phrase "just girls" followed my own work beyond my year of data collection. While I was in the process of writing up my research, I was called on several occasions to present in-service training on detection of sexual harassment in the public schools. When I argued that my research was not about harassment, the most common remark was, "but you're studying just girls, aren't you?" That girls presumably are tied to their sexuality in ways that boys are not is deeply problematic.

When one accesses library computerized searches, the key words "adolescent females" prompt a long list of materials that fit under one of two categories: sexuality and economics. Marketing for adolescent females is big business, and articles that document commercial trends and purchasing power dominate such reference lists. Sexuality is characterized by articles that focus on the victimization of adolescent women: promiscuity, pregnancy, sexual harassment, and rape. The adolescent female is reduced to two dimensions.

After presenting my research to a joint meeting of five reading councils, I asked participants to help me explore the implications for us as literacy educators. The first response from one teacher was, "It's biology. We can't fight biology in our classrooms. We're powerless to fight it." The next added, "It's economic. If a girl picks up a fifteen-dollar can of hair spray to get her bangs to stand up like that then the advertisers have done their job." A sense of powerlessness filled the room, and conversation died.

This conception of the adolescent female as tied to economics and sexuality is pervasive, yet such determinism denies the power of education. Left to their own devices, students have few options but to live out received scripts, invisible and impossible to revise. Literacy instruction can begin to make visible to students the roles that are presently available in our texts, in our classrooms, in our society. When we begin to examine the motivations behind particular publications, we begin to change those publications. Intentions need not govern receptions.

Whenever I hear the phrase "just girls," I never hear "only" girls, but an urgent command for justice for them in our schools and in our society. We need to follow the path of Chinese-American author Maxine Hong Kingston, who, in response to Bill Moyers' (1988) question, "Do you think you can change the world?" said without hesitation, "Oh, yes, and we do it word by word. . . . I change the language. I change people's mouths. I change the world."

References

American Association of University Women. (1992). *How schools shortchange girls: A study of the major findings of girls and education*. Washington, DC: AAUW Educational Foundation.

Apple, M. (1986). *Teachers & texts: A political economy of class & gender relations in education*. New York: Routledge.

Apter, T. (1990). *Altered loves: Mothers and daughters during adolescence*. New York: Fawcett Columbine.

Atwell, N. (1987). *In the middle: Writing, reading and learning with adolescents*. Portsmouth, NH: Boynton/Cook.

Bakhtin, M. M. (1981). *The dialogic imagination*. Austin: University of Texas Press.

Belenky, M. F., Clinchy, B. M., Goldberger, N. R., & Tarule, J. M. (1986). *Women's ways of knowing: The development of self, voice and mind*. New York: Basic Books.

Biklen, S., & Pollard, D. (1993). *Gender and education: Ninety-second yearbook of the National Society for the Study of Education*. Chicago: The University of Chicago Press.

Bourdieu, P. (1977). *Outline of a theory of practice*. Cambridge, UK: Cambridge University Press.

Bourdieu, P. (1991). *Language and symbolic power*. Cambridge, MA: Harvard University Press.

Brantlinger, E. (1993). *The politics of social class in secondary school: Views of affluent and impoverished youth*. New York: Teachers College Press.

Britton, J. (1970). *Language and learning*. London: Penguin Books.

Britzman, D. (1993). Beyond rolling models: Gender and multicultural education. In S. Biklen & D. Pollard (Eds.), *Gender and education: Ninety-second yearbook of the National Society for the Study of Education* (pp. 25–42). Chicago: The University of Chicago Press.

Brooke, R. (1991). *Writing and sense of self: Identity negotiation in writing workshops*. Urbana, IL: National Council of Teachers of English.

Brooks-Gunn, J., & Reiter, E. O. (1990). The role of pubertal processes. In S. S. Feldman & G. R. Elliott (Eds.), *At the threshold: The developing adolescent* (pp. 16–53). Cambridge, MA: Harvard University Press.

Brown, B. B. (1990). Peer group and peer cultures. In S. S. Feldman & G. R. Elliott (Eds.), *At the threshold: The developing adolescent* (pp. 171–196). Cambridge, MA: Harvard University Press.

Burke, K. (1990). Language and symbolic action. In P. Bizzell & B. Herzberg (Eds.), *The rhetorical tradition: Reading from classical times to the present* (pp. 1034–1041). Boston: Bedford Books of St. Martin's Press.

Cazden, C. (1988). *Classroom discourse: The language of teaching and learning.* Portsmouth, NH: Heinemann.

Cherland, M. (1994). *Private practices: Girls reading fiction and constructing identity.* London: Taylor and Francis.

Christian-Smith, L. (1993). *Texts of desire: Essays on fiction, feminity and schooling.* London: The Falmer Press.

Cintron, R. (1991). Reading and writing graffiti: A reading. *The Quarterly Newsletter of the Laboratory of Comparative Human Cognition, 13,* 21–24.

Coleman, J. S. (1961). *The adolescent society.* New York: Free Press.

Comer, J. P. (1993). The potential effects of community organizations on the future of our youth. In R. Takanishi (Ed.), *Adolescence in the 1990s* (pp. 203–206). New York: Teachers College Press.

Davies, B. (1989). *Frogs and snails and feminist tales: Preschool children and gender.* Sydney: Allyn and Unwin.

Delpit, L. (1988). The silenced dialogue: Power and pedagogy in educating other people's children. *Harvard Education Review, 58,* 280–298.

Delpit, L. (1991). A conversation with Lisa Delpit. *Language Arts, 68,* 541–547.

Dunning, S., & Stafford, W. (1992). *Getting the knack: Poetry writing exercises.* Urbana, IL: National Council of Teachers of English.

Dyson, A. (1992). The case of the singing scientist: A performance perspective on the "stages" of school literacy. *Written Communication, 9,* 3–47.

Dyson, A., & Freedman, S. (1990). *On teaching writing: A review of the literature* (Technical Report No. 20). Berkeley: University of California, Center for the Study of Writing.

Eagleton, T. (1991). *Ideology: An introduction.* New York: Verso.

Eccles, J., & Harold, R. (1993). Parent-school involvement during the early adolescent years. In R. Takanishi (Ed.), *Adolescence in the 1990s* (pp. 110–129). New York: Teachers College Press.

Eckert, P. (1989). *Jocks and burnouts: Social categories and identity in the high school.* New York: Teachers College Press.

Erickson, F. (1986). Qualitative methods in research on teaching. In M. C. Wittrock (Ed.), *Handbook of research on teaching* (3rd ed.) (pp. 119–161). New York: Macmillan.

Evans, E., Rutberg, J., Sather, C., & Turner, C. (1991). Content analysis of contemporary teen magazines for adolescent females. *Youth and Society, 23*(1), 99–120.

Everhart, R. (1983). *Reading, writing and resistance: Adolescence and labor in a junior high school.* Boston: Routledge & Kegan Paul.

Feldman, S., & Elliott, G. (1990). *At the threshold: The developing adolescent.* Cambridge, MA: Harvard University Press.

Finders, M. (1992). With Jix. *College Composition and Communication, 43,* 497–507.

Finders, M., & Lewis, C. (1993). Commentary. *Reading Today, 10,* 35.

Finders, M., & Lewis, C. (1994). Which parents care? Examining assumptions about parental involvement. *Educational Leadership, 51*, 50–54.

Fine, M., & Macpherson, P. (1993). Over Dinner: Feminism and adolescent female bodies. In S. Biklen & D. Pollard (Eds.), *Gender and education: Ninety-second yearbook of the National Society for the Study of Education* (pp. 126–154). Chicago: The University of Chicago Press.

Foley, D. (1990). *Learning capitalist culture: Deep in the heart of Tejas*. Philadelphia: University of Pennsylvania Press.

Freedman, S., Dyson, A., Flower, L., & Chafe, W. (1987). *Research in writing: Past, present, and future* (Technical Report No. 1). Berkeley: University of California, Center for the Study of Writing.

Gee, J. (1990). *Social linguistics and literacies: Ideology in discourses*. London: The Falmer Press.

Gilbert, P. (1988). Student text as pedagogical text. In S. DeCastell, A. Luke, & C. Luke (Eds.), *Language, authority and criticism: Readings on the school textbook* (pp. 195–202). London: The Falmer Press.

Gilbert, P. (1991). Writing pedagogy: Personal voices, truth telling and "real" texts. In C. Baker & A. Luke (Eds.), *Towards a critical sociology of reading pedagogy* (pp. 27–47). Philadelphia: John Benjamins.

Gilligan, C. (1982). *In a different voice: Psychological theory and women's development*. Cambridge, MA: Harvard University Press.

Gilligan, C. (1988). *Moral voice: Adolescent development and secondary education*. Cambridge, MA: Harvard University Graduate School of Education.

Gilligan, C., Lyons, N., & Hanmer, T. J. (Eds.). (1990). *Making connections: The relational worlds of adolescent girls at the Emma Willard School*. Cambridge, MA: Harvard University Press.

Gilligan, C., Ward, J., & Taylor, J. (Eds.). (1988). *Mapping the moral domain: a contribution of women's thinking to psychology and education*. Cambridge, MA: Harvard University Graduate School of Education.

Giroux, H. (1992). Critical literacy and student experience: Donald Graves' approach to literacy. In Patrick Shannon (Ed.), *Becoming political: Reading and writing in the politics of literacy education* (pp. 15–20). Portsmouth, NH: Heinemann.

Goffman, E. (1959). *The presentation of self in everyday life*. New York: Doubleday.

Goffman, E. (1961). *Asylums: Essays on the social situation of mental patients and other inmates*. Chicago: Aldine Publishing Company.

Goody, J., & Watt, I. (1963). The consequences of literacy. *Comparative Studies in Society and History, 5*, 304–26, 332–45.

Graves, D. (1983). *Writing: Teachers and children at work*. Portsmouth, NH: Heinemann.

Griffin, C. (1985). *Typical girls: Young women from school to the job market*. New York: Routledge.

Hall, G. S. (1904). *Adolescence* (Vols. I & II). Englewood Cliffs, NJ: Prentice-Hall.

Heath, S. B. (1982). Protean shapes in literacy events: Ever-shifting oral and literate traditions. In D. Tannen (Ed.), *Spoken and written language: Exploring orality and literacy, Vol. 9* (pp. 91–117). Norwood, NJ: Ablex.

Heath, S. B. (1983). *Ways with words: Language, life, and work in communities and classrooms.* Cambridge, UK: Cambridge University Press.

Hines, M. B. (1992). The dynamics of "difference": Teaching for social change. *Iowa English Bulletin, 40,* 10–21.

hooks, b. (1990). *Yearning: Race, gender and cultural politics.* Boston: South End Press.

Kamler, B. (1993). Constructing gender in the process writing classroom. *Language Arts, 70,* 95–103.

Klein, H. (1990). Adolescence, youth and young adulthood: Rethinking current conceptualizations of life stage. *Youth and Society, 21,* 446–471.

Lareau, A. (1987). Social class differences in family-school relationships: The importance of cultural capital. *Sociology of Education, 60,* 73–84.

Lensmire, T. (1994). *When children write: Critical re-visions of the writing workshop.* New York: Teachers College Press.

MacLeod, J. (1987). *Ain't no makin' it: Leveled aspirations in a low-income neighborhood.* Boulder, CO: Westview Press.

McRobbie, A. (1978). Working class girls and the culture of feminity. In Women's Studies Group (Eds.), *Women take issue: Aspects of women's subordination* (pp. 96–108). London: Hutchinson.

Meyers, J. (1992). The social contexts of school and personal literacy. *Reading Research Quarterly, 27,* 297–333.

Miller, R. (1994). Fault lines in the contact zone. *College English, 56,* 389–408.

Moss, G. (1995). Rewriting reading. In J. Holland & M. Blair (Eds.), *Debates and issues in feminist research and pedagogy* (pp. 157–168). Clevedon: The Open University.

Moyers, B. (Author). Public Affairs Television Corporation (Producer). (1988). *A world of ideas: Interview with Maxine Hong Kingston* [Videotape]. Alexandria, VA: Public Broadcast Service Video.

Olson, D. (1977). From utterance to text. *Harvard Education Review, 67,* 257–279.

Peirce, K. (1990). A feminist theoretical perspective on the socialization of teenage girls through *Seventeen* magazine. *Sex Roles, 23,* 491–500.

Pratt, M. L. (1991). Arts of the contact zone. In *Profession 91* (pp. 33–40). New York: MLA.

Radway, J. (1984). *Reading the romance: Women, patriarchy and popular literature.* Chapel Hill: University of North Carolina Press.

Richardson, P. (1991). Language as personal resource and as social construct: Competing views of literacy pedagogy in Australia. *Educational Review, 2,* 171–190.

Romano, T. (1987). *Clearing the way: Working with teenage writers.* Portsmouth, NH: Heinemann.

Sadker, M., & Sadker, D. (1986). Sexism in the classroom: From grade school to graduate school. *Phi Delta Kappan, 67,* 512–515.

Santrock, J. W. (1993). *Adolescence: An introduction.* Dubuque, IA: Brown and Benchmark Publishers.

Schlegel, A., & Barry, H., III. (1991). *Adolescence: An anthropological inquiry*. New York: The Free Press.

Scott, J. (1990). *Domination and the arts of resistance: Hidden transcripts*. New Haven: Yale University Press.

Scribner, S., & Cole, M. (1981). Unpackaging literacy. In M. F. Whiteman (Ed.), *Writing: The nature, development and teaching of written communication* (pp. 71–87). Hillsdale, NJ: Lawrence Erlbaum.

Shuman, A. (1986). *Storytelling rights: The uses of oral and written texts by urban adolescents*. Cambridge, UK: Cambridge University Press.

Shuman, A. (1993). "Get outa my face": Entitlement and authoritative discourse. In S. Hill & J. Irvien (Eds.), *Responsibility and evidence in oral discourse* (pp. 135–160). New York: Cambridge University Press.

Silverman, K. (1983). *The subject of semiotics*. New York: Oxford University Press.

Smith, F. (1986). *Insult to intelligence: The bureaucratic invasion of our classrooms*. Portsmouth, NH: Heinemann.

Spradley, J. (1979). *The ethnographic interview*. Forth Worth: Holt, Rinehart and Winston.

Spradley, J. (1980). *Participant observation*. New York: Holt, Rinehart and Winston.

Stretch, C. (1991). *From self-awareness to self-mastery: Literacy and the discourse of body consciousness in teen magazines*. Unpublished manuscript.

Szwed, J. (1981). The ethnography of literacy. In M. F. Whiteman (Ed.), *Writing: The nature, development, and teaching of written communication* (pp. 13–23). Hillsdale, NJ: Lawrence Erlbaum.

Takanishi, R. (1993). Changing views of adolescence in contemporary society. In R. Takanishi (Ed.), *Adolescence in the 1990s* (pp. 1–7). New York: Teachers College Press.

Taylor, T. (1987). *The cay*. New York: Doubleday.

Vygotsky, L. (1962). *Thought and language*. Cambridge, MA: Harvard University Press.

Vygotsky, L. (1978). *Mind in society*. Cambridge, MA: Harvard University Press.

Walkerdine, V. (1990). *Schoolgirl fictions*. New York: Verso.

Weiss, L. (1993). Disempowering white working-class females: The role of the high school. In L. Weiss & M. Fine (Eds.), *Beyond silenced voices: Class, race, and gender in the United States schools* (pp. 95–121). Albany: SUNY Press.

Wertsch, J. (1991). *Voices of the mind: A sociocultural approach to mediated action*. Cambridge: Harvard University Press.

West, C., & Zimmerman, D. H. (1987). Doing gender. *Gender and Society, 1, 2,* pp. 125–151.

Willinsky, J., & Hunniford, R. M. (1993). Reading the romance younger: The mirrors and fears of a preparatory literature. In L. Christian-Smith (Ed.), *Texts of desire: Essays on fiction, feminity and schooling* (pp. 87–105). London: The Falmer Press.

Willis, P. (1977). *Learning to labor: How working class kids get working class jobs*. New York: Columbia University Press.

Zebroski, J. (1989). The social construction of self in the work of Lev Vygotsky. *The Writing Instructor, 8,* 149–156.

Index

Academic achievement, 48
Academic drive, 72, 84
Adolescence
  and adult ties, 56, 122
  characteristics of, 13–14
  conceptual models of, 11–14, 121–123
  as culture, 18–21
  discourse of, 28–30, 55, 88, 115
  diversity and, 40
  early, 13–14
  and female victimization, 130
  myths about, 121–123
  and need for space, 28–29, 39–40
  paranoia in, 53
  transition into, 3–4
  zines as handbook for, 60–61, 65
Adult ties/resistance, 28–29, 43–44, 66, 84,
  98. *See also* Literate underlife
Adulthood, growth into, 45
Advertising, in teen magazine, 64–65, 130
Allegiance
  family, 85
  and intellectual engagement, 72–73
  literacy and social, 4
  and note-writing, 68–69
  and significant adults, 56, 84, 98, 122,
    129
  visibility of, 23, 43, 53–54, 68–69
  and yearbook signing, 43
Angie
  and book selection influence, 71
  and extracurricular activities, 37–38
  and free choice, 121
  life experience of, 50

and note-writing, 67
reading the zines, 56–57, 58–60
resisting distinction, 49
resisting intellectual engagement, 72–73,
  78, 79
and rest room graffiti, 69–70
and *Sassy* subscription, 61
as social queen, 21–22
Appearance, 48, 61. *See also* Fashion
Apple, M., 16
Apter, T., 11, 12
Atwell, Nancie, 27, 40, 118
Authority, 4, 43–44, 60–61, 63, 96–97, 98,
  127

Backstage
  girls' rest room, 69
  and Home Interiors party, 97
  interaction, 9–10, 54, 60
Bakhtin, M. M., 9, 18, 63, 96, 109, 127
Barry, H., III, 12, 13, 40, 86
Belenky, M. F., 16, 53
Belonging, sense of, 32, 34, 36, 39
Biklen, S., 12
Biological determinants, 11, 28, 121, 122,
  130
Book club, 78
Boundaries, 4, 23, 35–36, 66, 71, 87–88
Bourdieu, P., 37, 42
Brantlinger, E., 13
Britton, J., 10, 52, 65, 70
Britzman, D., 12
Brooke, R., 9
Brooks-Gunn, J., 2, 11, 121

Brown, B. B., 2, 11
Burke, K., 30, 116

Carrie, 49, 73, 79
Cazden, C., 10, 96
Center stage interaction, 9–10
Chafe, W., 9
Cherland, M., 41, 42
Christian-Smith, L., 3
Cintron, R., 18
Classrooms, 27, 116, 118–119, 126
Cleo
    academic focus of, 84
    assumptions of, 113
    boundary crossing by, 104
    exclusion from groups of, 85
    and free choice, 120
    and gender roles, 86
    and home/school dichotomy, 88–90
    ignoring of suggestions of, 100, 101
    issues papers and narratives by, 111–113
    Merlyn's Pen submission by, 102, 103
    peer groups and, 29, 103
    and privacy issues, 89, 103–104
    as reader, 99, 101, 102–104
    seeking critique by, 101, 102
    self–determination of, 83
    and teacher expectations, 113
    as tough cookie, 22–23
    as writer, 101–103, 111–113
    and yearbook, 35–37, 38–39, 47
    and zines, 58
Clinchy, B. M., 16
Clubs, 32–33, 45–47
Codes, 44, 66
Cole, M., 8
Coleman, J. S., 11, 121
Collaboration, 85, 95, 108, 114
Comer, J. P., 12, 29
Comfort, 27, 119, 123
Competition, 33, 41–42, 53–54, 94–95, 96
Confidentiality during research, 2
Contact zone and critical discussion, 126
Critical reflection, 101, 102, 123, 126
Crowley, Mary C., 93
Cultural capital, 37, 46, 47
Culture, shared, 36, 120
Curriculum
    coordinators, 7
    free choice and, 111

and planning literacy learning, 125–126
sociopolitical student relationships and,
    5
student-centered, 1, 26–27
tough cookies and, 115
yearbook and, 33

Davies, B., 12
Delpit, L., 123
Discourse
    of adolescence, 28–30, 55, 88, 115
    community, 3
    of student–centered pedagogy, 117
Diversity, 40, 43, 117
Dottie
    academic focus of, 84–85
    and competition, 94–95, 96
    direct response and, 113–114
    exclusion from groups, 85
    and gender roles, 86
    and Home Interiors party, 92, 94, 96
    and home/school dichotomy, 88–90
    and individual expression, 96
    and mother's literacy definition, 92
    and privacy issues, 98, 105–106, 107
    and social issues, 94
    and textbook authority, 98
    as tough cookie, 22–23
    yearbooks and, 37, 38–39
Dyson, A., 9

Eagleton, Terry, 46
Eccles, J., 29
Eckert, P., 11, 13, 88
Economic constraints, 36, 94
Economic ideology, 59, 61, 64, 97, 130
Elliott, G., 2, 11, 12
End-of-school activities, 33–34
Entitlement, yearbook signing, 43
Environment, nurturing, 116
Erickson, F., 3
Erikson, Erik, 11
Evans, E., 59, 64
Everhart, R., 1, 11, 77
Expectations, 23, 26–27
Extracurricular participation value, 33

Family, importance of, 39–40
Fashion, 48–49, 61. See also Appearance
Feldman, S., 2, 11, 12

Finders, M., 7
Fine, M., 12, 13
Flower, L., 9
Focal students, 2, 16–17, 118–119
Foley, D., 11, 77
Free choice, 5, 111, 120–121, 129
Freedman, S., 9
Freud,, Anna, 11
Friendship circles
  and coded notes, 66
  consensus in, 49
  in class, 14–16
  sanctioned literacy and, 72, 118
  and social queens, 20, 50–51
  visibility of, 2. *See also* Group identity; Social queens; Tough cookies

Gee, James, 3, 9
Gender marking, 41, 68, 86, 124–125
Gender role studies, 12–13, 123–125
Gilbert, P., 123
Gilligan, Carol, 12, 13, 16, 17, 53, 123
Giroux, H., 32
Goffman, Erving, 9–10, 24, 48, 54, 60
Goldberger, N. R., 16
Goody, J., 8
Gossip, 52–53
Graffiti, 4, 54, 56, 69–71
Graves, D., 27, 40
Griffin, C., 12
Group identity, 48–50, 80, 107–108
Group leaders, 2

Hanmer, T. J., 12, 16
Harold, R., 29
Heath, S. B., 3, 8, 10
Helpfulness, 25
Hines, M. B., 123
Home Interiors party, 92–96
hooks, b., 12
Hormones, 28, 122
Hunniford, R. M., 62

Identity kit, 3, 50
Ideology, 47, 59, 64
Inclusion, 119
Incomplete assignments, 38
Individuality, 50–52, 83, 85

Intellectual engagement, 72–74, 75–78, 111, 119, 123–124, 125
IRE lesson structure, 96

Jargon, 44–45
Junior high school, 7–8, 46, 56, 117
"Just girls," 17–18, 130–131

Kamler, B., 123
Kingston, Maxine Hong, 131
Kissing up, 77–78, 111, 119
Klein, H., 11

Language arts, 26–28, 40
Lareau, A., 13
Lauren
  and appropriate social roles, 55
  and free choice, 120
  and note–writing, 67
  as reader, 79
  and rest room graffiti, 69–70
  as social queen, 21–22, 50, 51–52
  and zine models, 61
  and zines, 56–57, 58–59
Lensmire, T., 1
Lewis, C., 7
Literacy
  and documenting social position, 23–24
  as event, 10
  learning in self-contained classroom, 129
  as rite of passage marker, 18–20, 57–58
  sanctioned, 24, 40, 45
  sociocultural, 126
  sociopolitical, 8–11
  text as authoritative, 127
Literacy club, 32, 69
Literate practices
  allegiances and, 5, 118–119
  documenting, 3
  in Dottie's home, 92–99
  and portfolios, 126
  and social boundary markers, 21
  and social roles, 5, 118–119
  and tough cookies, 90
  and transition from child to adult, 117
  and yearbook signing, 40–41
Literate underlife
  definition of, 1
  and freedom and independence, 129
  function of, 24–26

sanctioned literacy versus, 81
and sense of play, 54
and social queens, 55–71
and writing what cannot pronounce, 80
and yearbook signing, 40
Lyons, N., 12, 16

MacLeod, J., 12, 13
Macpherson, P., 12, 13
McRobbie, A., 40
Magazines, teen (''zines''), reading, 4, 54,
56, 57–58, 59–61, 62
Male-only studies, 11–12
Marketing, adolescent, 64–65, 130
Membership, social context and, 32, 45–46
Meyers, J., 32
Miller, R., 126
Moss, G., 127–128

Notes, 4, 54, 56, 65–69

Olson, D., 8
Outsiders, 44

Parents, 3–4, 63–64, 86, 129
Pedagogical and assessment strategies, 7,
116–117
Pedagogy, 1, 105, 108–109, 128, 129
sources of, 27
student-centered, 116, 118
student-negotiated, 126
Peers
culture model, 11
dynamics of, 5, 49, 77–78, 111, 119
groups, 28–29, 40, 85, 107–109
influence of, 49, 71, 83, 109, 110–111
Performance, staged classroom, 72
Performance teams, 48
Photographs, in student yearbook, 32, 33,
35–36
Pollard, D., 12
Portfolios, 126
Power relations, 4, 43–44, 119
Pratt, M. L., 126
Premenstrual syndrome (PMS), 25
Privacy, 85, 90, 105, 107, 114–115
Professional class, 7

Radway, J., 80
Reading, 1, 27, 48, 64

''Real girls,'' 17–18, 91
Recess, 25, 87
''Regular girls,'' 17–18
Reiter, E. O., 2, 11, 121
Research, 1, 116, 128–130
Residence, socioeconomic status of, 7
Resistance, 28–29, 43–44, 56, 66
Response
in groups, 107–108, 113, 120
personal, 5
Richardson, P., 123
Rite of passage, 18–19
Romance, 41
Romano, T., 27
Rules and rituals, 4, 66–67
Rutberg, J., 59

Sadker, D., 123
Sadker, M., 123
Safe haven, 116, 118–119, 126
Safety, pedagogical, 27
Sanctioned literacy, 24, 45
kissing up and, 77–78, 111, 119
literate underlife versus, 81
school, 71–79
and tough cookies, 91, 104–105
and yearbook signing, 40
Santrock, J. W., 11, 53
Sather, C., 59
Schlegel, A., 12, 13, 40, 86
School structure, 6–7, 17, 46–47, 115, 117
Scott, James, 10
Scribner, S., 8
Self
female sense of, 16–17
focus on, 46–47
multiple and shifting, 23
Self-reliance, 83
Sexual harassment, 42
Sexuality, adolescent female, 25, 42, 45,
69–71, 130
Sharing, 36, 111
Shuman, A., 12, 43, 44, 63
Smith, F., 32
Social interaction, 9–10, 105
Social network dynamics, 3, 12–14, 128
Social outings, 13, 17
Social queens, 20, 21–22
and criticism of one not present, 51, 52
and competition, 53–54

defying intellectual engagement by, 73–74
and group identity, 48–50
and kissing up, 77–78
and literacy use, 54–55, 80, 81
and note-passing, 68
and rest room graffiti, 69–71
and rewriting cultural, social scripts, 128
and sexual definition, 45
and yearbook, 36, 43, 45, 47
Social roles, 14–16, 48, 55, 128
Socioeconomic status, 6–7, 12–13, 36–37, 46–47, 62, 97
Spacers, 123–125
Spradley, J., 3
Status, 4, 43–44, 53, 58, 61, 67–68, 69–81
Stone, Mr., 14–16, 28–29, 84–85, 129
Storm and stress model, 11, 121–122
Stretch, C., 17
Student-centered pedagogy, 116, 118, 123
Student-negotiated pedagogy, 126
Szwed, J., 9

Takanishi, R., 12
Tarule, J. M., 16
Taylor, J., 12
Teacher preparation, 26–27, 117–120
Teacher-student interaction patterns, 28–29, 105, 123
Team membership, 33, 78
"Terministic screens" (Burke), 30, 116
Texts
    authoritative, 60–61, 63, 96–97, 98
    sociocultural shaping, 127, 128
Tibidioux, Rick
    and assessment of Lauren, 79
    and direct response to build community, 113
    and free choice, 120
    parody of, 44
    and pedagogical safety, 27, 119
    and power of peer influence, 49
    and reading aloud, 75
    and spacers in classroom, 124
    and Tiffany's behavior, 74–75, 76
Tiffany
    and appropriate social roles, 56
    "Creation of Big Red, The," 74–75
    and extracurricular activities, 37–38
    and free choice, 120

lateness of, 77
and note-writing, 67
as reader, 76
resisting distinction, 49
resisting intellectual engagement, 73–74, 75–77
response to grade on autobiography, 74–75
rest room graffiti, 69–70
as social queen, 21–22, 51–52
and yearbook, 34–35, 36, 47
and zines, 56–57, 58–59
Tough cookies, 20, 22–23
    adult approval and, 84, 96, 98
    and competition, 94, 96
    exclusion of, 36–37
    and home/school dichotomy, 88–90, 114–115
    and kissing up, 111, 119
    and privacy issues, 85, 90, 105, 107
    resist collaboration, 85
    rewriting cultural, social scripts, 128
    and school day and peer networking, 86–87
    and textbook authority, 98
    yearbook, 36–37, 39–40, 43, 47
    zines and, 58
Trailer parks, 7, 36–37, 85, 90
Turner, C., 59

Universal adolescent model, 13–14, 121

Ventriloquation, 109–110
Violence, symbolic, 42, 46
Vygotsky, L., 8–9, 108, 123

Walkerdine, V., 25, 123
Ward, J., 12
Watt, I., 8
Weiss, L., 40, 98, 115
Wertsch, J., 9
West, C., 41
Willinsky, J., 62
Willis, P., 12, 13
Winning, focus on, 46–47
Women's roles, 17, 97
Working class, 7, 40, 86
Writing, 1, 27, 48, 69, 105, 106–107, 126–127

Yearbook
  anticipation of, 31–32
  defacing of, 45
  gatekeepers of, 36
  inscriptions in, 41
  photographs, 32, 33, 34
  sales of, 33–34, 36
  and school district ideology, 45–47
  signing of, 33–34, 36, 40–45
  staff of, 35–36

Zebroski, J., 9
Zimmerman, D. H., 41

Zines. *See* Magazines, teen
Zmoleck, Debra
  and assessment of Tiffany, 76
  and gender differences, 53
  and hierarchical social sorting, 67
  and junior high teacher role, 29
  and peer influence, 83
  and reading, writing workshops, 27
  and social-group identity, 48
  and spacers in classroom, 124
  writing assignments, 111–113, 120
  and yearbook arrival, 33–34

About the Author

Margaret J. Finders is an Assistant Professor of English and Education at Purdue University, where she teaches language and literacy courses. She also collaborates with public school teachers as part of the School of Education's partnership with Professional Development Schools. A former junior high language arts teacher, her research focuses on early adolescence and sociocultural dimensions of literacy learning. She received her Ph.D. from the University of Iowa. Most recently, her work centers on teacher preparation for the middle grades.